The
Dixie
Dictionary

Your complete guide to the Southern Language

Edited by Thomas W. Howard

The Dixie Dictionary

Your complete guide to the Southern Language

Edited by Thomas W. Howard

SWEET WATER PRESS

This edition published for Sweetwater Press
by arrangement with Cliff Road Books.

ISBN 1-58173-204-X

Illustrations by Rodney Davidson

Printed in the United States of America

10   9   8   7   6   5   4   3   2   1

To my wife, Anne, and daughters Catherine, Judith, and Alice;

and to writers and editors everywhere who share a love of the

Southern language.

Introduction

A Congressional subcommittee holding hearings on bilingualism in the United States heard experts on the pros and cons of educating the young in Spanish, African, or one of the Asian languages in addition to English. One language not discussed, however, was that of the traditional American South.

It is time somebody spoke on behalf of preserving it, and *The Dixie Dictionary* seeks to do just that. This book also is intended to help visitors or new residents of the southeastern part of the country to comprehend what the natives are saying.

The Southern language is more than just an accent or a dialect. It is a rich verbal tradition of descriptive words and phrases, a wealth of expressions and colloquialisms.

Language is nothing more than communicating with words, sometimes standing alone but usually connected together. Dictionaries serve as a general record of a language, for both written and spoken aspects. A dictionary is based on current and past usage, some common, some rare. Many of the words in this dictionary were founded in the past, while others are the creations of the present.

Because the people of the South claim primarily European or African origins, the roots of many Southern words are in the English, Welsh, Scottish, Irish, German, and African languages. Thus, Southerners need not feel they have to defend their language. In fact, dictionaries generally have claimed that words are defined and established through their use. And Southerners use the Southern language.

For those who dwell in other parts of the United States, the South is a place where people "talk funny." Millions of Southerners will dispute this—not counting the additional millions of Americans, mostly in the western United States, whose forebears migrated from the South in the 18th and 19th centuries.

To understand the Southern language it is necessary first to understand the manner of speech in the region. Much of it was verbalized first and written later. As Europeans populated the South, farming communities remained relatively self-sufficient, without a great deal of commerce and cultural exchange from beyond. Words and phrases developed and spread slowly. However, in the last six or seven decades, during and following World War II, the transformation has been dynamic. People have left the farms and mountain hollows and moved into towns and cities. They have migrated throughout the South and beyond.

Many of the words, phrases, and expressions included in *The Dixie Dictionary* stem from the days of those small communities, but now their usage has spread far and wide—some regular, some uncommon. The language is defined by its accents and dialects, which is why entries in this dictionary are spelled phonetically, as a Southerner might utter them, so that users can look up the spelling of a word as they have heard it.

But if you are not a Southerner, remember the cardinal rule: Don't ever try to imitate a Southern accent, at any time, at any place, on any occasion. Not even outside of the South. You never know when or where there will be a closet Southerner in your midst.

Another excellent reason for this rule is that there is no standard Southern accent, so no matter what you say or write, or how you say it, it is likely to be wrong. Linguistic researchers have been at work for years to identify a common denominator, but although they agree the South is a definite "speech region," no single Southern accent or drawl fits all. The honey drawl of South Carolina is completely different from the drawl heard in the uplands of Georgia. The soft speech tones of Virginia are not those of east Texas. The languid accents of Mississippi and Alabama are distinguishable instantly from the lilting accents heard in the mountains of Tennessee.

Such a forest of myths surrounds the Southern language that it's difficult to know where to start chopping to make a reasonable clearing. For example, there is a quaint notion alive in the northern part of this country that people in the South speak more slowly due to the heat and humidity. Of course, that's absurd. If this were so, Southerners would talk faster in the winter than they do in the summer. Or people in the northern part of the South, say Virginia and Kentucky, would be linguistically speedier than Mississippians. Likewise, if there were any merit to such a claim, other people of English descent who live in hot and humid climates elsewhere in the world also would speak more like Southerners, which they don't. The great-great-grand-children of English settlers of Nairobi in East Africa, Sydney in Australia, and the Canadian Maritimes don't say things like "y'all," "kiss my grits," and "sho' 'nuf."

Another wheezy old myth is that the English language of the South is the residue of Oxford University perfection, brought to the Southern colonies centuries ago and somehow frozen in isolation. A twist on this myth is that there are isolated mountaineers in the hollows of the Appalachians who speak "pure" Elizabethan English. There may have been a time this was so, but they aren't there now. With the advent of pickup trucks and paved roads, there aren't many places in the South out of reach of a Wal-Mart store, a television set, and other American cultural influences.

Linguists have reached some conclusions, though. They believe the speech of the South's coastal areas resembles that of the eastern counties of Britain. In general, the speech of the lower South has been deemed closer to that of London and the southern counties of Britain. Hill country dialects have been compared to those of the north of Britain, Scotland, and Northern Ireland, the brief ancestral lodgings of the breed known as the Scotch-Irish.

Unfortunately, nobody knows for sure what those accents sounded like. There were no tape recorders, and linguistic scholarship was not as advanced as it is today. Nevertheless, modern linguists have declared the South to have more diversity of speech than any other region of the country, so we will leave it at that.

Certain phonetic and grammatical features of the Southern language do need explanation because they are so common. For example, a lot of people worry about how many Southerners drop the letter *r*, such as at the end of *beer*, which sounds like "beah." But there's no harm done. All the *r*s dropped in the South get shipped to New England where they are added to words that never were intended to have any, such as "idear" and "Americur."

Some Southerners use double-modal or multiple-modal construction, such as "might could," "may can," and "might should," as in: "I might could get straight As if I didn't have to chop all that cotton." You also will find the word *done* used to create emphasis, as in: "I done told you that, but you still gotta chop the cotton."

There is a prevalent use of "liked to," meaning "almost," as in: "I liked to died out there chopping all that dadblamed cotton."

Also heard is the prefix, *a-*, with verbs ending in *-ing,* as in: "Boy, you keep on a-talking like that, and I'll get you a-walking back to the cotton patch."

Newcomers to the South should not worry about variations in speech patterns. They might hear something one place, go a hundred miles away and not hear it, then go another hundred miles and pick it up again.

Linguists have identified a couple of language regions within the South. The first is the coastal zone from Virginia to Texas, or lowland Southern. The second is the South Midland, covering the Piedmont, the southern Appalachian mountains from Virginia through South Carolina, the hill areas of Georgia and

Alabama, and touching into mountain areas of Tennessee, Kentucky, and the Ozarks. In other words, the South has lowlanders and highlanders, an important distinction to remember.

In a broad sense, this matches up with the migratory patterns of the early colonists, who moved into the tidewater ports of the upper South and then down the coast. Later arrivals moved in from ports farther north, traveling south through the Shenandoah Valley and along the Piedmont. This is no small point in understanding the whole Southern character and accent. There was a major accent boundary from the outset between the tidewater and lowlands, and the hill and mountain country. It still exists.

A century or more ago, the urban centers of Charleston, Savannah, and Richmond, all in the lowlands, had extraordinary influence throughout the South. But today, the newer metropolises of the South are Charlotte, Nashville, Louisville, and Atlanta. All in the hills and close to the mountains, these are the dynamic centers for linguistic changes and regional standards of speech.

There you have it. The highlanders are winning out over the lowlanders. The thrifty Scots are eating the lunch of the lazy English. The lowlands have been the domain of the Southern snob, the slothful plantation cretin who believes social customs are more important than hard work.

The highlanders are a separate breed of Southerner. The hills and mountains were settled by independent farmers, who didn't call their farms plantations because they were about a tenth of the size. Many thought slavery deserved to be outlawed and raised their own field hands. They were brought up to think anybody who lived down in the flats by the sea was a grasping, insufferable aristocrat who deserved to have his beard pulled.

It is unclear when the speech of the South became distinctive. The first lexicographers in the United States were mostly New Englanders, and they had no interest in studying the

Southern language. They didn't like what they were hearing in the South and said so. They actually were the first ones who said Southerners talked "funny."

So is anything changing the Southern language today? The answer: an emphatic yes. It has changed dramatically in the past fifty years, due to television and more education. There was a fear in some circles that the national broadcast media stars with their standardized nondescript manner of speech would homogenize the accents of the South, but there is little evidence this has occurred.

There is a small threat from speech classes that help Southerners lose their accents. A tidal wave of criticism has enveloped some of these when they have become publicly known, but this is a teapot tempest. For many years Southerners who travel north for employment have been changing their accents to fit the occasion.

A Southerner is nothing if not adaptable. This has been so for decades. Many have a repertoire of two or more different styles of speaking, depending on the audience and the occasion. If a Mississippian moves to New York, she will alter her speech for New Yorkers, then shift back to her native dialect in an instant when talking to other Southerners. A politician knows instinctively when to switch from his cocktail party accent to his backshop accent when shooting the breeze with a bunch of the good ol' boys.

The Southern language is primarily verbal, because Southerners are born talking. The art of conversation is an inherited gene. In the old days when people had front porches, they grew up swinging and rocking in the evenings, talking with their families and neighbors. The invitation to "come on up and set a spell" was the diploma of acceptance.

This devotion to the oral tradition has left the Southerner with at least one built-in advantage over the rest of the folks in this country: He or she knows when and when not to believe

Southern political rhetoric. It comes as a great surprise to Southerners when, after hearing a political speech given by a well-known Southern orator, they learn that political analysts and northern-based political strategists actually are taking the orator seriously. The Southern listener knows that most of it sounds great, but it is just so much hot air. He holds dearly that the truth is to be found in what the speaker does, not in what he says. This probably sums up the difference between North and South. The North thinks that saying is doing. The South knows that just isn't so.

The richness of the Southern language is displayed in every aspect of life in the region. Take monsters. The South has had monsters in the form of goblins and frightful creatures for several centuries, all lurking out there in the heavy timber and swamps and marshes. In one form or another, monsters have been the essence of bedtime stories, and they have thrived in the lore spread furtively around campfires by many a gathering of Southern primitives. Doubters say these monsters were concocted to scare children so they wouldn't run away, or to explain what happened to nosy revenue agents who went where they weren't wanted and never returned.

For example, the dreaded Bingbuffer is a beast that kills animals and people by throwing stones with its hinged tail. He has turned up in almost every Southern state in each century. Almost as popular is the Giasticutus, a legendary bird with a fifty-foot wingspan that can carry off a fully grown cow for its supper.

Down in the piney woods of the deep South stalks the Whistler, a fabled black panther that lures timber workers to their doom by whistling at them from cedar thickets. A similar monster is the Wowzer, a super panther that bites off the heads of livestock.

Other such creatures are the fabled Wampus Kitty, the Side-Hill Hoofer, and the Whiffle-Bird. The Wampus Kitty is a bloodthirsty animal thought to patrol the wilds, while the

Side-Hill Hoofer runs around the mountain tops, always in the same direction because its legs are longer on one side than the other. The Whiffle-Bird is a legendary fowl that always flies backwards, much like the Bogie-Bird.

Another topical area where the language shows its colloquial affluence is in how Southerners describe each other. Lest non-Southerners feel they are being singled out in being treated with contempt, there is a history of disdain between Southern city folks and Southern country folks. Country folks traditionally have been mocked as everything from flint busters, acorn-crackers, briar hoppers, and bush busters, to weed benders and fruit jar suckers. Depending on the region, they are called hay shackers, hog rangers, puddle jumpers, and pumpkin rollers. Other times they are referred to as ridge-runners and sorghum lappers, sprout straddlers and squirrel-turners. Mountaineers are called, not kindly, mountain boomers, brush apes, and, if they are from North Georgia, wool-hatters. Yahoos and yokums are foolish countrymen who are swindled by fast-talking city boys. You might think country folks have been the losers, but that isn't the way they look at it. Country people bask in the kind of equanimity born of the conviction that they have the good life and others are just plain envious.

The rivalries between states can get caustic. A laplander, for example, is not a Scandinavian but a person who lives on the Missouri-Arkansas border. A man who has his trousers stick to his body during hot weather is said to be suffering from North Carolina heartburn. A slab of salted roe-herring is referred to as a North Carolina robin. A Rackensack is an Arkansan. A razor-back hog is known as a Carolina racehorse. A roach is a Charleston butterfly, and a buzzard is a South Carolina eagle.

Arkansas has been especially vulnerable. A dirt road is referred to as Arkansas asphalt. A chamber pot is called an Arkansas fire extinguisher. Salt pork is known as Arkansas chicken, and cornbread is Arkansas wedding cake.

Southern wit hasn't excluded Europeans. To a tobacco farmer, a Frenchman is a spindly plant of useless quality. Someone who has stepped in a cow patty is said to have cut his foot on a Dutchman's razor.

Moonshine whiskey is known variously as fox-head, bald face, tanglefoot, coon dick, field whiskey, and stump-water whiskey. Gator-sweat is homemade hooch that has been buried in the ground for five years to age. Kill-devil is poor whiskey. Kill Devil Hill on North Carolina's Outer Banks was reportedly the home of some fine outlaw whiskey merchants. Brush-arbor whiskey got its name because it was sold to people who attended camp revivals, or brush-arbor revivals. A pocket-pistol is a small liquor flask. A tickler is a small bottle of whiskey, containing just enough to tickle. If you add too much water to your bourbon, you drowned the miller.

Satan is more than just the Devil. He's also known as Old Harry, Old Nick, Old Boy, Old Red, Old Rip, Old Sam, Old Coaley, Old Ned, the Dark Stranger, Harry Scratch, Old Scratch, Old Horny, Old Blackie, Old Samson, and Old Jimson.

And there is a full range of terms for infants. A lap-baby is one old enough to sit in a lap, a knee baby is one just walking and clutching at mama's knees, and a waist baby is one tall enough to reach to her waist.

An illegitimate child is referred to as a Sunday baby, a wood's colt, a yard-child, a blackberry baby, a briar patch child, an alley cat, or an ash-barrel baby. A sooner is a child born less than nine months after a wedding. A woman who has broken her leg has had a child out of wedlock.

A loose woman may be called a fan-foot, a hussy who brazenly seeks men's favors. She also goes by the terms shag-leg, trapes, alley bat, drabbletail, and hoe.

A chicken is called a gospel bird because it was the main dish served on Sunday when the minister came to dinner after services. A pokeweed religion is a fervent one lacking staying power. Tent revivals are known as lightning bug revivals because they go out quickly. Toadstool churches are storefront churches run by lunchbreak parsons. A stump-knocker is a traveling preacher.

These terms are the heritage of the Southerner. The once-isolated mountain hollows now are filled with well-appointed homes of retirees from Minnesota and New York. The shores of once-remote tidal hamlets from Virginia to Texas are inhabited with commuter residents who have high-tech jobs in nearby cities. Native Southerner or northern transplant, they need to know about Bingbuffers, Carolina heartburn, and stump-knock-ers. This dictionary is dedicated to helping them find out.

The Dixie Dictionary

- A -

abanded *adj* : abandoned
abear *v :* to abide or bear
able *adj* : wealthy
abode *n* : a wooden plank <If
  you hit him up side the head
  with ~ he might listen.>
aboon *adv* : thinking of oneself as superior
about give out *phr* : tired or
  exhausted <I ran over here
  so fast that I'm ~!>
abouten *adv, prep,* or *adj* :
  about <There's something ~
  that girl I can't figure out.>
abroad *adv* or *adj* : said of a
  trip beyond the community
abscond *v* : to hide or conceal
  <Make her show you the
  money before she ~s it.>
ackenpucky *n* **1:** any food
  mixture of unknown ingredients **2:** a food of jellylike
  consistency, such as gelatin
acknowledge the corn *phr*
  1: to confess or own up to
  something **2:** to admit that
  one is at fault or outdone
acorn-cracker *n* : a country
  rube

across the tracks *phr* : on the
  poor side of town
acrost *adv* or *prep* : across
act like you are somebody
  phr **1:** to have some pride in
  yourself **2:** to show what
  you're worth
act up *v* : to misbehave
Adam's ale *n* : water
Adam's housecat *phr* : <I
  wouldn't know him from ~.>
adays *adv* **1:** by day
  2: during the daytime
addle **1:** *adj* rotten **2:** *v* to
  confuse
adopt *v* : to contract, usually
  an illness
afeard *adj* : afraid
affidavy *n :* affidavit
afflicted *adv* : feebleminded,
  mentally off kilter
afore *adv, prep,* or *conj* :
  before
Africky *n* : temper or dander
aftertimes *adv* : later
again *adv* **1:** by **2:** by the
  time **3:** before
agen, agin *adv* **1:** again
  2: against **3:** before <~ I can
  do that, he will be gone.>
agg *n* : egg
aggerpervoke, **aggervex**,
  aggravoke *v* **1:** to irritate or
  annoy **2:** to provoke

aggie forties *n* : anything very strong; usually said of a drink

aginer *n* : one who is against

aglee *adj* : gleeful

agley *adj* : morally gone wrong

agnail *n* : a hangnail

agony, agony pan *n* : a vessel used to hold fermenting fruit during wine-making

ague, ager *n* : fever —*Var* buck ager, buck ague, buck eggers, dumb ague

agwine *v* : going

agy *adj* : aged

ahint *adv, adj,* or *prep* : behind

ahmlode *n* : an armful or armload <Don't leave without getting an ~ of flowers.>

aholt *n* : a hold <Grab ~ of the reins and don't let go.>

ahoo, ahuh *adv* : crooked or lopsided, awry

ah tay yah *phr* : I tell you!

aidge *n* : edge

ailded *v* : sickened

ailish *adj* : sick

aim to *v* : intend to

ain't fittin' *phr* : not right, especially used to describe improper behavior

ain't got a grain of sense *phr* : stupid

ain't got a lick of sense *phr* : stupid

ain't got enough sense to come in out of the rain *phr* : stupid

ain't got no *phr* : has no reason to

ain't much *phr* **1:** bad off <She ~ these days.> **2:** sort of trashy <She sure ~.>

ain't no place in heaven or hell *phr* : nowhere to go

ain't only *phr* : not only

ain't right *phr* : mentally lacking <That boy ~.>

ain't worth killing *phr* : said of a person of little consequence

air **1:** *v* are <~ you going to town?> **2:** *n* hour <It's about an ~ from here.> **3:** *adv* there <Look up ~!>

airish *adj* : cool, airy

airly *adj* : early

airn **1:** *v* to earn **2:** *adj* not one, nary

airy *adv* : any <I ain't seen ~ one.>

airyfied *adj* : inclined to put on airs

al *n* : owl

alemand *n* : a dance call, as in a square dance

alewife *n* : a fish, member of the herring family

all *n* : oil <His car's in need of about three quarts of ~.>

all atwitter *phr* : twittering

all broke up *phr* : distressed <She's ~ about losing her job.>

all by my lonesome *phr* : all by myself

allers, allus *adv* : always <He's ~ late.>

alley bat *n* : immoral woman

alley cat *n* : illegitimate child

all fire *phr* : hell fire

all fired *phr* : extremely <What's yore ~ hurry?>

all fours *phr* : on hands and knees

all git out *phr* : to the extreme <Don't that beat ~?>

all hat and no cattle *phr* : said of someone in Texas who is all show and of little substance

all heeled *phr* : well provided for, doing all right, well heeled

all my born days *phr* : since I was born

all over creation *phr* : something that is everywhere

all overs *phr* **1:** nervous **2:** underwear

allowed *v* **1:** to declare **2:** to intend

alls *n* : all one's belongings <We packed our ~ and moved out of that place.>

all spruced up *phr* : washed and dressed in one's best clothes

all the *phr* : the only <He's ~ friend I've got.>

all the fast *phr* : as fast as, the fastest

all tore up about it *phr* : something very upsetting <I heard the bad news and I'm ~ .>

all vine and no 'taters *phr* : said to describe someone who is all talk and no action

all wool and a yard wide *phr* : said to describe someone who is first class, genuine

alongst *prep* **1:** along **2:** through **3:** by the length of

alter *v* : to castrate

ambeer *n* : tobacco spittle

amen corner, amen row *n* : front row in church, place where devout kneel at a revival

ammon *n* : almond

ammonia coke *n* : dash of ammonia in Coke for headaches and anxieties

amongst *prep* : among

amount to something *phr* : become successful

ancient *n* : a flag

and that's a fact *phr* : for sure

angleworm *n* : earthworm

angleworm

anigh *adv* : near

ankle-biter *n* : small child

ankle express *phr* : going on foot

anoint *v* : to whip something, used sarcastically

ant-bug *n* : ant

antick *adv* **1:** playful, fresh **2:** sometimes wild or ungovernable **3:** *n* : a clown, buffoon

antigodlin *adv* : askew, not parallel to something having well-established lines

anti-gagglin, anti-ganglin, antigodlin, antigoglin *adv* : diagonal, diagonally

antney over *n* : game played by throwing a ball over a house —*Var* antony over, anty over

antses *n* : ants

antymire *n* : ant

anxious bench *n* : bench in the front of the church near the pulpit for people who want to pray or be prayed for

anyhow gone *phr* : gone for sure <She took the baby so she must be ~ .>

anyways *adv* : anyhow, anyway

apern, aporn *n* : apron <I'm glad to see the cook has her ~ on.>

apiece *adv* : an undetermined distance <He lives down the road ~.>

a piece of my mind *phr* : a verbal dressing down <I'm gonna give her ~.>

aplenty *n* : a lot

appearantly *adv* : apparently

appintedly *adv* : assuredly, positively

apple knocker *n* : a rustic person

apple peeler *n* : knife

applicate *v* : to pester one with requests <That feller just ~s me morning, noon and night.>

a purpose *n* : on purpose <That was no accident, he tripped me ~.>

arbuckle *n* : a sore, boil

arction *n* : auction

a'ready *adv* : already

argufy *v* : argue

argy *v* : argue

Arkansas asphalt *n* : a dirt road

Arkansas chicken *n* : salt pork

Arkansas fire extinguisher *n* : chamber pot

Arkansas toothpick *n* : a Bowie knife, a large sheath knife, a dagger

Arkansas wedding cake *n* : cornbread

Arkansaw *v* **1:** to cheat, take advantage of **2:** to sweep out **3:** to go dutch on a meal

arky *adv* : archaic

armstrong *n* : a crude, primitive tool or implement

arn *v* : earn

arn *n* **1:** iron **2:** a shooting iron or gun

arnins *n* : earnings

arnj *n* : orange, citrus fruit

arns *n* : andirons

Arsh *n* : Irish <I shore like them ~ taters.>

arsle *v* : to back out <I didn't like the offer so I ~ed out.> —*Var* azzle

arsters *n* : oysters

arter *adv* : after <One thing ~ another.>

ary *adv* : any <I ain't seen ~ one of them.>

arything *n* : anything

as *adv* : that, who, which <Them ~ thinks they can.>

ash-barrel baby *n* : illegitimate child

ash cakes *n* : corn cakes baked before an open fire

ashcat *n* : child who plays in ashes, a dirty child

ash hopper *n* : a wooden trough used to make lye from ashes

ashy *adv* : provoked, angry, ill-tempered

a sight of *n* : a lot of something <She's picked ~ berries.>

as mad as a pig on ice with his tail frozen in *phr* : plenty mad

as mad as a rooster in an empty henhouse *phr* : some kind of mad

as much chance as a one-legged man at an ass-kissing contest *phr* : no chance at all

aspersed *v* : slandered

ass in a sling *phr* : dejected, beaten down by circumstances

ass licker *n* : sycophant, yes-man

as sure as God made little chickens *phr* : no doubt about it

as sure as God made little green apples *phr* : very certain

ast *v* : ask, asked

a'tall *phr* : at all, of all

at himself, herself *phr* **1:** in good health **2:** at one's best

A to izzard *phr* : completely <That teacher learned us everything from ~.>

attaboy *phr* **1:** praise, encouragement **2:** contraction of <That's a boy.>

atter *adv* : after

auger-eyed *adj* : sharp-eyed, gimlet-eyed

auntie *n* : old black woman

auto *v* : ought to <You ~ go home.>

awf *adv* : off <Turn ~ the light.>

awfullest *adv* : worst of all

awmos *adv* : almost

awork *adv* : lively with motion <The net was ~ with fish.>

ax *v* : ask —derived from old English

- B -

Babble *n* : Bible

baby *n* : youngest member of the family, regardless of age

baby catcher *n* : midwife

baby clouts *n* : baby clothes

baby trough *n* : cradle, play pen

baby waker *n* : firecracker

baccy *n* : tobacco

bachelor's button *n* : a wooden peg used as a button

back *v* **1:** to mount a horse **2:** to address a letter <Are you gonna ~ that letter?>

back and forth *v* : to work in an aimless or futile manner

backdoor trots *n* : diarrhea

backed up *n* : constipation

backfin *n* : prime crabmeat

back gap *n* : alley

back jaw *v* : talk back to

backset *n* : setback

backside of the moon *phr* : any place that is remote

back-staff *n* **1:** a support **2:** substantial evidence

back talk *n* : sass, impudent response

bad disease *n* : syphillis

badman, buggar-man *n* : the devil

bad mouth *v* : speak ill of someone

bad off *adj* **1:** poor **2:** sick

bad place *n* : hell

bad sick *adj* : very ill

baid *n* : bed

bail *n* : bell

baird *n* : beard

bait *n* **1:** a large amount, usually of food **2:** bet **3:** bit

baited for women *phr* : dressed to kill, used of a male

bait worm *n* : earthworm

baker *n* : a cooking utensil used for baking biscuits or cornbread

bald *n* : bare mountain top

bald face *n* : raw corn whiskey

balks *adj* : sulking, stubborn

balks *n* : box

ball **1:** *n* bullet **2:** *v* to boil, also bawl

balled *v* : boiled

ballet *n* : ballad, old song

ball naked *adv* : completely naked

ball the jack *v* : to move swiftly

banded up *phr* : bandaged up

bandy *v* : move about

banger *n* **1:** great falsehood **2:** large person

bank barn *n* : barn built on sloping ground

banker *n* : one who lives on North Carolina's Outer Banks

banter *v* : to dare

bantling *n* : a child

bar *v* : borrow <I'd like to ~ your lawnmower.>

bar *n* : bear

barbed wire pie *n* : any disagreeable or offensive thing

bard *v* : borrowed

bare *n* : beer

barefoot bread *n* : hard cornbread, made with just corn meal and water, without eggs or shortening

bare naked *adv* : naked

barking dogs *n* : sore feet

barking up the wrong tree *phr* : misinformed <He's ~ on that one.>

barley *adv* : barely

Barlow *n* : type of knife, named after Russell Barlow who invented it

barn *v* : born

barn door's open *phr* : a man's fly is open

barning *n* : harvesting, usually of tobacco

barnyard preacher *n* : part-time preacher, not ordained

barrel into *v* **1:** to shoot into **2:** to run into

barter *n* : butter

baseborn *n* : illegitimate child

basket meeting *n* : picnic of church or social group

bastard oak *n* **1:** a variety of oak **2:** cross between ordinary black oak and blackjack oak **3:** a white oak used to make baskets

bat *n* : woman of ill repute

bat *v* : wink, shut your eyes

bate *v* : bet

bateau *n* : flat-bottom boat

batter bread *n* : cornbread without eggs, also with eggs

batter cake *n* : pancake

battlin' stick *n* : club that pioneer women used to beat their clothes in washing

baubee, bawebee *n* : a trifle, something of small value

bawlin' hound *n* : baying hound

bear a hand *v* : lend a hand

beast back *adv* : riding bareback

beat all *v* : surpasses expectations <That just ~.>

beat around the bush *v* : to be vague, evasive; to avoid the point

beat down *adv* : feeling low or depressed

beat-out *adv* : worn out

beaten biscuit *n* : biscuit made from kneaded dough

beatenest *adj* **1:** finest, very exceptional **2:** unusual

beats picking cotton *phr* : an easier task or job

beaucoup *n* : an abundance of something

Beulah land *n* : heaven

beauticious *adj* : facial beauty

becausen *conj* : because

be dawg it *phr* : be darned

bed baby *n* : baby that cannot crawl yet

bed clothes *n* : sheets, pillowcases, blankets, covers

bedcord strong *adv* : very strong indeed, as in the cord used in old bedsteads

bedpost chillun *n* : small children confined by placing a bedpost on part of their garments

bedrid *adv* : bedridden

bed rug *n* : counterpane, bed spread

bed spell *n* : period before bedtime

bee-all *n* : all that is to be

bee gum *n* : beehive

beeler *n* : wooden maul used in splitting rails, a big mallet

been to the bushes *phr* : used the toilet

beggar lice *n* : small seeds of a field weed that stick on pants and socks

beggar-trash *n* : low class, usually said low-class whites

begone *adv* : leave

begouge *v* : to stab, pierce

beholden *v* : indebted

belch back *v* : rebound, but usually unfavorably

believe you me *phr* : said to emphasize a point <~, I ain't going with them at any time.>

belling *n* : ceremony after a wedding (in mountains)

bell-tail *n* : rattlesnake

belly-rub *n* : almost any dance

belly wash *n* : soda pop

belong *v* : should, ought, to be supposed

benighted *v* : to be overtaken by darkness

bereft *adj* : crazy

berlue *n* : noisy racket among children

Bermoothes *n* : Bermuda Islands

berryglaumer *n* : person who can pick strawberries very rapidly

bespoke *v* : asked for, promised

best *adv* : better <You'd ~ not do that.>

bestest *adv* : the very best <He's the ~ they is.>

best good *adv* : the best

best most *adv* : utmost

Betsey, Betsy *n* : a term of endearment applied to various tools and utensils

betsey bug *n* : any sort of large dark-colored beetle found in rotten wood

better had *v* : had better

betty *n* : chamber pot

between hawk and buzzard *n* : the twilight hour

betweenst *prep* : between

between the rock and the hard place *phr* : a dilemma without a lot of solutions

betwixt *prep* : between

beyonst *prep* : beyond

bibble *v* : drink like a duck

Bible Belt *n* : the deep South

bidaciously *adv* : bodaciously

biddable *adj* **1:** obedient **2:** docile

biddie *n* : call for a chicken

biddies *n* : baby chicks

bidness *n* : business

big as all outdoors *phr* : immense

big church *n* **1:** the devil's church **2:** no church

big daddy *n* : grandfather

big dog *n* : conceited, pompous person

big doins' *n* : an affair of unusual importance or size

Big Easy *n* : New Orleans

big-eye *n* : be greedy, covetous <He put the ~ on my pie.>

the biggest half *n* : the majority, most

biggety, biggity, briggity, brickety *adv* : conceited, proud, haughty, stubborn, snobbish

big house *n* **1:** manor house **2:** refers to living room apart from the smaller kitchen

Big Ike *n* : a self-important person

big mama *n* : grandmother

big money *n* : a lot of money <He made hisself some ~ on that deal.>

big road *n* : any public road

big time *n* : a good time

big-to-do *n* : an occasion of some importance, sometimes used derogatorily

big'un *n* : big one, as an incredible story

bile *v* : boil

billy-maria *n* : a country dweller

bimeby *phr* : by and by

binding *v* : causing constipation

biney *n* : a goblin, bugaboo

Bingbuffer *n* : a fabulous beast said to kill other animals by throwing stones with its hinged tail

binny *n* : belly, usually of a child <The baby has a ~ ache.>

birding *v* : singing a part in a song

bird-wire *n* : thin wire with a weight on one end, used to cast into a covey of quail

bird-work *v* : to leap forward, to progress by a series of stiff-legged jumps

biscuit weather *n* : snowy weather

bishop *n* : a woman's bustle

bitch kitty *n* : bad tempered girl <She's a real ~ when she's hungry.>

bitch's baby *n* : a bad situation

bitch-wolf *n* : a standard hyperbole <I'm hungry as a ~.>

bitey *adj* : biting

biting frost *n* : a killing frost

bitsy bit *n* : small amount

bitty, bittle *adj* : small

blabber *n* or *v* : babble, chatter

blackberry baby *n* : illegitimate child. —*Var* blackberry patch baby

blackberry winter *n* : late cold spell in May or early June when blackberries are blooming

black bottom *n* : low-lying section of town inhabited by blacks, sometimes on land by the river

blackguard *v* : to use vulgar or obscene language, to tell smutty stories

blackleg *n* : gambler

black strap molasses *n* : very dark, strong molasses

blade *n* : wife

blame, dadblame *adj* : an oath <If I could have I would have kicked that ~ cat to kingdom come.>

blanket-stretcher *n* : a teller of tall tales, also wind-jammer, windy-spinner

blanny *n* : blarney

blast, blasted *adj* : oath, as in blast darn, blast damn

blate *n* : bleat, as a sheep

blather *n* : bladder

bless out *v* : scold, rebuke

blind pig *n* : a speakeasy during Prohibition

blink *v* : sour

blinked *n* : slightly sour milk

blinky *adj* : slightly sour, as in milk

blinky-blue *n* : sour skimmed milk

bloat *v* : blowed

blobber-lipped *adj* : thick lipped

block and fall *n* : block and tackle, pulleys with rope or cable used to hoist or pull heavy objects

bloober *n* : blueberry

blood shotten *adj* : blood shot

bloody bones *n* : a boogeyman

blossomed out *v* : filled out <Boy, Mary Jo sure ~ since last winter.>

blow *n* : boaster

blow-down *n* : tree blown down by a storm

blowed *v* : blown, blew

blowgum *n* : bubble gum

blown up like a toad *phr* : said of someone who is very angry, seething, usually silently

bluebelly *n* : a Yankee soldier during the Civil War, now any Yankee

blue darter *n* : small chicken hawk

blue devils *n* : low spirits, delirium tremens

blue hen's chickens *n* **1:** local aristocracy **2:** quick tempered

blue john *n* : skimmed milk

boaging *n* : long stride

boar-cat *n* : tom-cat, male cat

board tree *n* : oak that is straight grained, suitable for splitting into clapboards or shingles

boat tide *n* : a freshet sufficient to float laden boats

bobble *n* : a mistake

bobtail *n* : dishonorable discharge from the army

bobwire *n* : barbed wire

bocks *n* : string beans

bodacious *adj* : outright, bold, brazen

bodaciously *adv* : boldly, wholly, altogether, out and out —*Var* bardaciously, bidaciously, bondaciously

bogue *v* : to move slowly, aimlessly about

bogue around *v* : wander aimlessly, restlessly and nervously

bohunkus *n* : rump

bolden *v* : to swell

bollsprit, bosplit, bowsplit *n* : bowsprit

boll weevil weather *n* : cold, wet weather

bone *v* **1:** study hard **2:** born

bone idle *adv* : lazy, wilfully and incurably indolent

bonnet *n* : small porch, sometimes only the roof of the porch

Bonnie Blue flag *n* : secession flag of South Carolina

booboo *n* : a cut, sore, or bump

boody *n* **1:** sexual intercourse **2:** a woman's sexual organs

booger *n* : baby, term of affection

booger *n* : demon to frighten children, haunt-ghost; also a louse

boogerboo, boogerman *n* : demon, goblin

booze *n* : liquor. Some believe it derives from a Kentucky distiller named Booze

boo up *v* : to praise

bore for the simples *phr* : a jocular phrase that a hole should be drilled in the head of someone who is joking around to let out the foolishness

born days *phr* : life <In all my ~, I haven't seen that.>

born on crazy creek *phr* : stupid <You think I was ~?>

born tired and raised lazy *phr* : said of someone who is without any drive

boss *n* : any white man, especially an employer of a Negro

boss dog *n* : top dog, person in charge

boss-man *n* : man in charge

bothen *pron* : both, as in <~ of you>

botherate *v* : to bother

botherment *n* : trouble

bottle drink *n* : a soft drink

bottom dropped out *phr* : a heavy rain

boughten *v* : to have bought something

boundary *n* : a tract of standing timber

bounden *adj* : under legal or moral obligation

bow-dark *n* : a long-growing tree widely planted as hedges; an Osage orange

boweevil *n* : boll weevil

bowel off, bowelling off *v* : have diarrhea <He was ~ something fierce.>

bowel rack *n* : cut or wound in which the intestines are exposed

bowels *n* : feces, dung

box picker *n* : guitar player

boy *n* : name for a male black servant, no matter what age. Regarded as highly offensive

boy *v* : buy

brack *n* : break, crack, flaw

brag bitch *n* : mistress

brag dog *n* **1:** favorite pet **2:** object of pride; sometimes of children

braggadocious *adj* : boastful

braid *n* : a loaf of bread

branch *n* : brook

branch water *n* **1:** trifling, shiftless **2:** pure natural water

branch-water folks *n* : people who camp anywhere and drink surface water

bran fire new *phr* : absolutely new —*Var* brand-spanking new

brang *v* : brought

brass ankle *n* : person of mixed race, a mulatto

brawl *v* : broil

brawling *n* : additional amount given for good measure

bray *v* or *n* : brew

bread-jerker *n* : Adams' apple

bread-wagon *n* : a thunderclap

break a leg *phr* : pregnant and unmarried

breakdown *n* : a riotous dance

breaking it off in someone *phr* : to hurt with a cutting remark

breaking up housekeeping *phr* : getting a divorce

break one's arm *phr* : self boastful

breast baby *n* : nursing baby —*Var* knee baby, lap baby

breath harp *n* : harmonica

breathing image *n* : resembles in appearance

breck *v* : break
brer *n* : brother
bresh *n* : brush
bresket, breskit *n* : energy
briar hook *n* : a scythe or sickle, also called briar blade
briar hopper *n* : country dweller, hillbilly
briar patch child *n* : child born out of wedlock
brickle *adv* : brittle, crisp
brile *v* : broil
brim *n* : bream, a fish
brinnel *adj* : brindle, a gray or tawny color streaked with a darker color
britches quilt *n* : quilt made out of heavy woolen fabric
britches riding high *phr* : said of someone who is proud and boastful
britchin's *n* : diapers
broad-hoe *n* : hoe with a blade a foot wide for weeding corn
broad-spoken *adj* : using coarse language
brogue *v* : to lounge, idle, or snoop around
broken her leg *phr* : with child, usually said of an unmarried woman
broken stick *n* : an unreliable person

bronical *adj* : bronchial
brook *adj* : broke
broomstick *n* : wife
broomstick marriage *n* : living together out of wedlock
brooze *v* **1:** wander about **2:** go about purposefully
brother *n* : common form of address of men in many Southern localities
brothren *n* : brethren
broughten *v* : brought, imported
brought-on *adj* : imported, foreign, ready-made, not homemade
brouse *v* : cohabit
bruck *adj* : broke
brung *v* : brought
brung-on *adv* : newly arrived, imported
Brunswick stew *n* : stew made from lima beans, corn, tomatoes, other vegetables, squirrel, and/or chicken. May originate in either Virginia or Georgia
brush, bresh, brash *n* : backwoods
brush *v* : whip with a switch or brush, punish
brush ape *n* : hillbilly

brush-arbor whiskey *n* : cheap but potent moonshine sold to people who attend camp revivals and brush-arbor or outdoor revivals —*Var* popskull, foxhead

brush drug *n* : crude seine made of willow boughs

brush mover *n* : a heavy rain

brush rack *n* : a raft or platform of small sticks tied together

bub *n* : bulb

Bubba *n* **1:** a young male **2:** brother **3:** used in large families for an oldest son

bubby *n* : woman's breast

buck-eye 1: *v* to poison **2:** *n* root of buck-eye tree, used to poison fish

buckhead *n* : a person of mixed race

buck like a colt *phr* : to object stongly

buck load *n* : a large drink of liquor

buck nekkid *adj* : nude

buckra *n* : a white man, usually in authority

bucks *n* : books

budget *n* : parcel, package <He was carrying a ~ of clothes under his arm.>

buffalo *v* : beat with a firearm

bugalug *v* : move about in an aimless way

bug-eater *n* : a worthless person

bug-eye *n* : a small boat with a triangular sail

bugger *n* **1:** term of endearment for a child **2:** dried nasal mucus **3:** a louse

bug hunting *v* : rub a person's nose in the dirt

bug scuffle *n* : a small town

buhr, burr *n* : millstone

build a pigpen *phr* : to deceive someone, or to cheat a customer. A woodcutter built firewood piles in shape of pigpens to make the load look larger

built from the ground up *phr* : well-built

bull-bat *n* : a night hawk

bull butterfly *n* : head man, stud

bulldocia *n* : boastful and threatening language

bull goose *n* : leader, boss

bull-wooley *n* : coarse, homespun clothes of cotton and wool

bully *n* : large marble

bullyrag *v* : to banter or abuse

bum *n* : bomb

bum *n* : buttocks

bumblefooted *adj* : awkward

bumblings *n* : adulterated whiskey

bumbo *n* : liquor made of rum or gin, sugar, water, and nutmeg

bumby *exp* : bye and bye

bumfidgets *n* : case of nerves

bum fodder *n* : toilet paper

bumfuzzle *v* : to confuse, perplex, be bumfuzzled

bump *v* : custom of punishing someone late for a fox-hunt (at sunrise) by bumping his backside to a tree while held by four men

bump *v* : to jump or excite bass, forcing them to jump in the boat

bun *v* : burn

bung bellies *n* : black-eyed peas or cornfield peas

bungersome *adj* : clumsy

bunk *n* : talk for talk's sake

bunnet *n* : bonnet

bunny hop *n* : side road

burdock *n* : coarse weed, used as a common remedy for gout, fever, eczema, and rheumatism

burgoo *n* : a rich stew

burial clothes *n* : best clothes set aside for burial

burial money *n* : cash or insurance to bury oneself. There was an old-time fear among poor Southerners that if there wasn't enough money for their burial, their bodies would be claimed by medical students

burned his britches *phr* : spanked

burnout *n* : destructive conflagration

burnt out on *v* : tired, sick of

burro *v* : borrow

buryin' *n* : a burial

bush baby *n* : illegitimate child

bush buster *n* : hillbilly

bush colt *n* : illegitimate child

bush up *v* : hide

bushwhacker *n* **1:** member of a guerrilla band **2:** someone who cuts across country through fields or woods

bussein *adj* : affected with a rupture or hernia

bussy *n* : sweetheart

buster *n* : a crab about to shed

busthead *n* : cheap liquor

busty *adj* : self-assertive, loud, boisterous

butter beans, buttah beans *n* : lima beans

butternut *n* : dye made from nuts from the butternut tree; commonly used to color fabric a yellowish brown. Southern troops in the Civil War dyed their clothes butternut when their uniforms wore out

butternuts *n* : brown overalls

butt-headed *adv* : stubborn or hard-headed

but what *phr* : but could be <I don't know ~ he's right.>

by-blow *n* : illegitimate child

by guess and by God *phr* : something more or less at random, without any accurate measurement —*Var* by guess and by golly

by jacks *interj* : an expression of surprise

by juckies *interj* : an expression of surprise

by the skin of his teeth *phr* : a narrow escape

- C -

cacky *n* : human excrement

caddow *n* : quilt, coverlet

caddy *n* : box or trunk

caigy *adj* : cautious

cain't hardlies *phr* : impatience <He's got a bad case of the ~.>

cain't hardly *phr* : cannot

Cajun *n* : Southern Louisiana residents who are descendants of French-speaking people who were deported by the British from Acadia in Canada in the mid-1700s

calaboose *n* : small-town jail

calcilate *v* : calculate

calico *v* : pass one's time with the ladies

calk *n* : cork

call **1:** *n* a desire **2:** *v* to recall, remember

caller *n* : collar

call hogs *v* : to snore

callyhooting *adj* : moving fast

cam *n* : calm

camphor *n* : camp fire

candy *adj* : candid

candy ass *n* : sissy

candy-breakin' *n* : a social game with men and women in pairs biting opposite ends of taffy candy

cane beer *n* : beer made from skimmings of boiling sugar cane juice. Can be very potent

canebuck *n* : liquor

cane chew *phr* : can't you

canecutter *n* : large swamp rabbit

cank *v* : to annoy, fret, overcome

canker *v* : to become tainted, to decay

canner *n* : an old cow

can-see to cain't-see *phr* : from dawn to dusk

cap'n *n* : captain, often used as a courtesy title

captain *n* : dapper young man who delights people with his suave manner

captain of the corn pile *n* : worker who walks on top of the corn pile at corn-shucking and leads the singing and hollering

carcass *n* : person's body <Park your ~.>

Carolina racehorse *n* : a razor back hog

Carolina robin *n* : smoked herring

carpet *n* : in the field to get married <He's on the ~.>

carpetbag *n* : large suitcase made of red carpet, also called carpetsack

carpetbagger *n* : any Yankee in the South. Derives from Reconstruction period when northern fortune seekers came south carrying their possessions in a carpetbag

carried away *adj* : excited about something <She's just ~ with the thought of going to New York.>

carry *v* : to tote, to take

carryings-on *n* : mischievousness, sometimes could be immoral

carry on *v* : act improperly

carry on a chip *phr* : to humor, pamper, spoil

cartons *n* : curtains

Carolina racehorse

case *n* : something else <He's a real ~.>

case knife *n* : table knife

cash money *n* : ready money

catamount *n* : bobcat

cat-and-clay *n* : rude chimney made of sticks and mud

catch air *v* : to leave fast

cat fever *n* : fever with a respiratory infection

catfish row *n* : usually a section of town occupied by poor blacks

cat-hammed *n* : horse with very crooked legs

cat heads *n* : biscuits

cat-hole *n* : very deep place in river, creek, or lake

cat-mint *n* : catnip

cat on a hot tin roof *phr* : someone ill at ease

catooch *n* : cartridge box

cat stepping *v* : walking quietly

catting around *v* : fooling around

cattle *n* : kettle

cat tongues *n* : long, slender, small oysters

catty-bias *adj* : in a diagonal position

cattymount *n* : fearful creature

cattywampus *adj* : in a diagonal position, awry

caught *n* : cot

caught short *v* : become pregnant out of wedlock

caul *n* : a sign of prosperity

The Cause *n* : the Confederate rationale of the Civil War

cave *n* : cellar

cawked *v* : exhausted

ceased *v* : deceased

chain gang *n* : gangs of prisoners chained together to work on roads while under guard

chainy *n* : china

chair *n* : cheer

chamber lye *n* : urine mixed with other ingredients as a medicine

cha-muck-a-muck *n* : relish of highly-seasoned mixed pickles

chance *n* : an amount of something

chancey *adv* : lucky

change-up *n* : change

channel cat *n* : catfish

chap 1: *n* baby, child **2:** *v* to have children

charge it to the dust *phr* : disregard for a debt —*Var* charge it to the sand

charge one's mind *v* : to burden one's mind with something

Charleston butterfly *n* : a roach

Charleston eagle *n* : a buzzard

charmber *n* : chamber

charmber-lye *n* : urine

charn *n* : churn

chartered whiskey *n* : whiskey strained through charcoal; good whiskey

chaunk *v* : to crunch or crush between the teeth

chaw *v* : chew

chaw-bacon *n* : countryman

chawed rosum *n* : something conspicuously excellent

chawed up *v* : embarrassed

chaw tobaccy *n* : chewing tobacco

cheapwad *n* : cheapskate

cheat *v* : term used in square dancing meaning to feint or swing <~ or swing>

cheer *n* : chair

chess *n* : chest

chew bubble *n* : bubblegum

chewed *v* : defeated

chew the rag *phr* : idle conversation

chew your own tobacco *phr* : rely on yourself

chicken feed *n* : trifling

chicken money *n* : pocket money from selling chickens

chicken ranch *n* : brothel

chick nor child *phr* : said of a woman who has no children and lives alone <She has nary ~.>

chile *n* : child

chill bumps *n* : goosebumps

chilrun *n* : children

chimbley *n* : chimney, also chimley, chumley

chimbley corner law *n* : self-made law

chimley crook *n* : a hook on old chimneys, a chain to hang pots

chinchy *adj* : stingy

chine *n* : backbone of a hog cut for cooking

chink *n* : money

chin music *n* : light chatter of no consequence

chinning *n* : talking

chips and grindstones *n* : odds and ends

chirrun *n* : children, also chern, churn, cheern

chit *n* : a pretty girl

chittlins *n* : chitterlings, small intestines of hogs, eaten when fried or stewed

chittlin' strut *n* : a social event during hog-killing time

choaty *adj* : fat, chubby, used to describe chubby children

choke rag *n* : necktie

choon *v* : chewing

choose *v* : to desire, care for

chop *v* : weed or thin crops, to hoe

chopfallen *adj* : dejected, dispirited, sullen

chouse *v* : to cheat, swindle

chub *n* : sweetheart, lover

chucklehead *n* **1:** dunce, large or thick head **2:** blue catfish

chuffy *adj* **1:** plump **2:** blunt, rude, surly

chug *n* : slight depression in the road

chug full *adj* : chock full

chune *n* : tune

chunk, chonk *v* : throw

chunk-floater *n* : heavy rain

churched *v* : expelled from a church

churm *v* : churn

churn *v* : to beat, drub, paddle

chutch *n* : church

cipher around *v* : to loiter about, get in people's way

citireen *n* : old resident, old timer, old fogy of either sex

civvy-cat *n* : civet or polecat

clabber *adj* : cloudy

clabber cheese *n* : cottage cheese

clabberhead *n* : foolish person, also foul-mouthed

clamb *v* : climb

claphat *adj* : hasty

clatterwhack *n* : chatter

clay eater *n* **1:** person who eats clay **2:** poor whites

clean *adv* : completely <I ~ forgot to go.>

cleanly *adv* : clean

clean one's plow *phr* : beat someone in a fight, to handle roughly <I cleaned his plow.>

clean out *adv* : go at once

clear across *phr* : clean across, all the way

clearing *n* : a social gathering

clever *adj* : good natured, friendly, hospitable, polite, generous —*Var* cleverness

clew *v* : to strike

clew bird *n* : fabled heron that sticks its bill in a sand bar and whistles through its rectum

climb one's frame *phr* : to attack or scold someone

clinker-built *adj* : said of a boat built with overlapping planks

clod-buster *n* : a heavy rain

clod-knocker *n* **1:** heavy shoe **2:** a countryman

close *n* : clothes

closet-drinker *n* : anyone who drinks on the sly; Baptists mainly

clothespress *n* : large wardrobe for hanging clothes

cloud *n* : a Negro

clout *n* : diaper

clumb *v* : climb

coal oil *n* : kerosene

coast *v* : cost

coasting coat *n* : hunting or coursing coat

coat *n* : court

cobbing *n* : vigorous rubdown with a corn cob soaked in grease or ointment

cobbing board *n* : wooden paddle

cobble up *v* : hastily throw together

cock of the roost *n* : boss, leader

coddle *v* : boil gently, to stew

cods *n* : testicles

coffin money *n* : burial insurance

coffin nail *n* : cigarette

coggled-up, coggly *adj* : rickety

cohee *n* : any Virginian living west of the Blue Ridge —*Var* coohee, from Scottish "quo he"

coined *adj* : kind

cole *adj* : cold

cold *v* : called

cold-cock *v* : hurl or fling in a decisive manner

cold drink *n* : a soda (Does not mean cold beer)

cold-harbor *n* : a protection at a wayside for travelers who are overtaken by darkness, a shelter, a lodging place. May stem from the Romans

cold out *adv* : for certain

cold overs *n* : leftovers

cold pimples *n* : goosebumps

cold potato *n* : dull person or thing

colonel *n* : salutatory nickname. May stem from colonial times, when county militia was headed by the most important landowner, who was given the title. Used today by the elderly for young boys

combustion *n* : a tumult, noisy agitation

come across *v* : to occur to

comeatable *adv* : that may be reached, attained or promised; capable of being approached

come back again *phr* : an invitation to a customer or guest to return <Y'all ~, y'heah.>

come bad *v* : to acquire a venereal disease

come-by *v* : to obtain, to come to have (as in inherited traits)

come by chance *n* : illegitimate child

come here *n* : someone not born in a county

come in *v* : to calve

to come out at the big end of the horn *phr* : to be successful

come through *v* : to accomplish something

come-too-soon *n* : a child born less than nine months after a couple is married

come to the end of one's row (rope) *phr* : run out of patience

come up *phr* : weather coming

come uppance *n* : an advantage, also a pay back

comical *adj* : peculiar

coming along *phr* : in one's early years <When I was ~, we didn't do it that way.>

commence to *v* : to begin or start

common *adj* : ordinary; derogatorily applied to people or behavior one doesn't approve of

common as pig tracks *phr* : said of people who are white trash or worse

commons *n* : provisions

Conch *n* : native of the Florida keys

Confederate beef *n* : mule meat

congealed salad *n* : gelatin salad with fruit or vegetables

congy *n* : congee, a bow or courtsey

conjure 1: *n* a supernatural spell **2:** *v* to deal in magic or supernatural spells

conohany *n* : hominy cooked with meats and nuts, seasoned with wild herbs

conniption fit *n* : a fit of anger

consarn it *phr :* an expression of irritation

consumpted *adj* : having tuberculosis

contrary *adj* : stubborn, hard-headed

cooche *interj* : said when calling chickens. Contraction of <come chick.>

coodle *n* : terrapin

cooling board *n :* large board used to lay a dead person on before rigor-mortis

coon *v* : to crawl around on all fours

coon *v* : to pilfer

coonass *n* : Cajun (a vulgar term)

coon dick *n* : a highly potent alcoholic drink, also coon juice

coon dog *n* : hound trained to hunt raccoons

coon-footed *adj* : pigeon-toed

coon's age *n* : a long time

coo-sheep *interj* : a call to sheep —*Var* coo-sheepy, coon-nan, coo-nannie

cooter   **1:** *n* turtle, terrapin   **2:** *v* to travel about aimlessly

copasetty *adj* : fine, excellent

Copperheads *n* : northerners who sympathized with the South in the Civil War

cordwinder *n* : shoemaker

cordwood *n* : a sign of rustic or rural breeding <A man with ~ on his breath has marks of backwoods origins.>

cork high and bottle deep *phr* : drunk

corncracker *n* **1:** very poor farmer **2:** primitive grist mill

corn dodger, corn pone *n* : corn bread in small loaves, hard cake of cornbread, a dumpling of cornbread

corn house *n* : corn crib

corn song *n* : a song sung at corn-shucking

corn squeezin's *n* : moonshine whiskey

corn to sell *phr* : said of a person who stands with his hands behind him

corn-wagon *n* : a thunder clap

corrupted *v* : ruptured

cotton *v* : agree <I don't ~ to what you want to do.>

cottonhead *n* : a towheaded child

cotton pickers *n* : field hands during cotton harvest

couldn't hit a bull in the ass with a bass fiddle *phr* : said of an inept person

could talk a cat out of a tree
phr : said of someone who is very persuasive

count *v* : to consider, regard

counterpane *n* : bedspread

country mile *n* : an indefinite distance

court *n* : cast

covering the water front *phr* : all inclusive

coverlid *n* : counterpane, bed-spread

cowcumber *n* : cucumber

cow-grease *n* : butter

cow itch *n* : trumpet vine, also known as bugle vine

cow peas *n* : blackeyed peas

cow pie *n* : cow dung

cow pound *n* : cow pen

Cracker *n* : a native of Georgia or Florida

cracklin' bread *n* : corn bread with cracklings

cracklings *n* : boiled meat rinds

cranberry merchant, busy as *phr* : very busy

crank-sided *adj* : lopsided

crap, craw *n* : crop <My corn ~ this year was hurt by the drought.>

crawdad, crawdaddy *n* : crawfish

crawdad *v* : crawl on one's belly like a crawfish

crawdad bottom *n* : swampy land usually too wet to culti-vate

crawl one's frame *v* : scold

crawly *adj* : infested with bugs

crazy as a peach-orchard pig *phr* : wild crazy person

cream gravy *n* : gravy made with fat, flour, cream, or milk

cream-pitcher *n* : a fish of the sucker family, also called a hog perch or hog-molly

creel *v* : to wrench or pull off <I ~ed that board off the fence.>

creen *v* : turn partly around and look

creep-mouse *n* : game of tickling babies by moving fingers along body like a mouse

creepified *adj* : scary

creeses, creasy greens *n* : cress or cress greens

crib basket *n* : stout basket made of oak splits

crimp up *v* : writhe in agony, collapse from pain

crimpy *adj* : cool, chill

cringle *n* : telephone pole insulator

crocus sack, croker sack *n* : burlap bag

crooked as a barrel of fish hooks *phr* : very dishonest

crope *v* : crept

cropper *n* : sharecropper

crossed up *v* : disagree

cross-jaw *v* : to chatter

cross-jostle *v* : to wrangle

cross my heart and hope to die *phr* : a statement made to prove the veracity of a claim

crow *n* : groove in top of barrel into which top is fitted

crow-bait *n* : worn-out horse

crowd the mourners *v* : to act prematurely, to show unseemly haste

crowner *n* : coroner

crud *n* **1:** skin disease **2:** a name applied to anything that makes one feel ill

crumb snatcher *n* : small child

crumbled in *n* : biscuits in sweet coffee

crumb-up *n* : corn bread crumbled in sweet milk

crupper *n* : buttocks

crusses *n* : crusts

cuckle *n* : cuckold

cull list *n* : the unwanted or undesirable <He's on her ~.>

cup *n* : coop

cupboard love *n* : insincere love professed for the sake of gain

cuppen *n* : cow pen

cup towel *n* : dish towel

curchy *n* : curtsey

curious *adj* : polite way to say someone is strange

currying *n* : sharp reprimand

curtain *n* : window shade

cush, coosh *n* : mixture of eggs, water, and leftover cornbread, fried in bacon grease

cuss-fight *n* : verbal quarrel

cut *n* : a piece of arable land enclosed by ditches

cut a big gut *v* : to do something foolish, to make oneself ridiculous

cut a foot *v* : to step into cow dung

cut a rusty *v* **1:** show off **2:** play a prank

cut a shine *v* : perform an action or gesture in a striking style or manner

cut a stick *v* : run rapidly

cut jackets *n* : a game in which two boys take turns hitting each other across the shoulders with a hickory stick. One who gives up first is loser

cut mud *v* : make haste

cut the buck *v* : move rapidly, as in a car

cut the comb *v* : to humiliate, abase

cut the fool *v* : behave stupidly

cut the short dog *v* : to caper, frisk around when tipsy

cut the tail off the dog *v* : cut it short

cutty hole *n* : small room or corner for storing plunder

cut your own weeds *v* : mind your own business

cyar *n* : car

cymlin *n* : any small gourd

cymlin-head *n* : a fool, a dunce, a gourd-head

cypress knee *n* : root growth of a cypress tree

- D -

dabblin' pan *n* : wash basin

dad burn it *phr* : an expression of frustration

daddy *v* : to father a child, usually out of wedlock

daggle *v* : to trail in the dust

daggly *adj* : wet

daid *v* : dead

daisy *n* : potato

dance juber *v* : leap wildly about

dank *v* : put on, apply

daresent *v* : not dare to do a thing

daresome *adj* : afraid

darken the door *phr* : a negative used to mean a person is not wanted <Get out of here and don't darken my door ever again.>

darnful *adj* : gloomy

dauncy *adj* **1:** lacking appetite, fastidious about food **2:** be in poor health, squeamish, fastidious, dizzy, sickly

day bust *n* : dawn

daylights *n* **1:** eyes **2:** consciousness <He beat the ~ out of him.>

daze *n* : days

dead on one's feet *phr* : to be very tired, exhausted

dead man *n* : inedible part of a crab

deadrise *n* : a small boat built up from a keel with a nearly flat rise

deadwood *n* : advantage, control with incriminating evidence <I've got the ~ on him.>

deah *adj* : dear

dearisome *adj* : very dreary, gloomy, forlorn

deed and double *interj* : son of a gun

deedeyedo *interj* : indeed I do

deef *adj* : deaf

delicum squinton *n* : whiskey

Delta *n* **1:** a stretch of rich, alluvial soil in Mississippi. Traditionally cotton country, the Delta is about 200 miles long and 60 miles wide **2:** the bordering lands around the mouth of the Mississippi River

derby *n* **1:** young foxhound **2:** derby dog (under 17 months) and derby gyp (female under 17 months)

devil's darning needle *n* : a praying mantis —*Var* called a devil's riding horse

devil's lane *n* : area between two fences built by farmers who can't agree on a common boundary

devil's riding horse *n* : praying mantis

dew poison *n* : athlete's foot, other rashes attributed to the toxic action of dew on the bare skin; also called ground itch

diarrhea of words *phr* : talkative

dib, dibby *n :* small chicken

dibble *v* : to dandle, as a child

dicty Negro *n* : a mulatto trying to pass as a white person

diddle *v* : copulate

diddly-squat *n* : something of little value. See also doodly-squat

dido *n* : a rowdy prank or exuberant caper

dift *v* : to strike, usually with the fist

dike up *v* : get dressed up

ding-dong *v* : to annoy

dinge *v* : to become dingy or murky

dingus *n* : a small article

dinky **1:** *n* dinghy **2:** *adv* neat or trim <His house is ~.>

dinnah *n* : dinner; usually the mid-day meal

dinner on the ground *phr* : outdoor picnic served at religious or musical gatherings

dint *v* : didn't

dip **1:** *v* use snuff **2:** *n* sweetened cream, syrup **3:** tobacco in molasses

dippy *n* : gravy

directly *adv* : in a little while

disciver *v :* discover

disencourage *v* : discourage

disfurnish *n* : inconvenience

disgust *v* : have a distaste for

dismals *n* : gloom, melancholy, dumps

disrecollect *v* : to forget, fail to remember, disremember

disremember *v* : not remember

dizzies *n* : a dizzy spell

dobbin' *n* : mud chinking between logs of an old-time cabin

doctoo *n* : doctor

doddle *v* : to move, raise, shake

doddly *adj* : nervous, shaky, unsteady

dod drot *n* : a mild oath

dodge times *n* : odd moments, spare time

do for *v* : provide help <She goes out of her way to ~ him.>

dog *v* : dug

dog fall *n* : a tie, usually applied to a wrestling match

dogged *interj* : darned <~ if I know.>

doggery *n* **1:** a grocery **2:** a saloon

dog-hair *v* : to grow slender, by reason of too much crowding <We planted them oats too thick and I'm afraid they're going to ~ on us.>

dog-leg fence *n* : rail fence built zig-zag

dog-pelter *n* **1:** term of contempt **2:** law officer of low rank

dog-run, dog-trot *n* : covered passage between two parts of a double log cabin

dogs, dog-irons *n* : andirons

dog-stud *n* : husband of a woman who has no children

dogwood winter *n* : cold spell when dogwoods are blooming

do-hickey *n* : term for substitute as name of something <What's that ~?>

do-less *adj* : lazy, inactive, slothful

done-in *adj* : sickly, exhausted

doney *n* : girlfriend, sweetheart, also a <doney gal>

donk *n* : alcohol, strong spirits

donnick *n* : a stone, usually one small enough to be thrown or used as a weapon

don't *v* : often added for emphasis in negative terms <~ never do that.>

don't amount to a bucket of spit *phr* : worthless person or thing

don't you fret none *phr* : don't worry

doodle *n* **1:** a rounded heap or pile, sometimes a cone **2:** a boil or a carbuncle

doodle-ant, doodle-bug *n* : a fuzzy-looking insect

doodly-squat *n* : something of little or no value <She ain't worth ~.>

dorts *n* : sulks

doty *adj* : decayed or rotten, also doted

double cousins *n* : the offspring of a brother and sister

dough *n* : door

down *v* : to plant <She's out ~ing the potatoes.>

down-face *v* : to contradict flatly

down in the mouth *phr* : despondent <He's been ~ lately.>

down the country *v* : to scold

drabble *v* : to draggle, make dirty, also wet and befoul

drabbletail, draggletail *n* : a woman with slovenly habits

draft *n* : a brook, small stream

drag *v* : to tease, twit

draggy *adj* : slow, tardy

dram *v* : to ply with drink

drammer *n* : a moderate drinker

drank *n* : drink

drap *n* : drop

draw *n* : drawer, as in a chest

draw *n* : small creek

draw a bite *v* : to prepare a meal

draw an idea *phr* **1:** to perceive **2:** to infer **3:** to decide

draw up *v* : shrink

drean *n* : a small stream of water, a small ditch

dreen *n* or *v* : drain

dreggy *adj* : foul, muddy

dremp *v :* dreamed

dress down *v* : scold

drinlin *adj* : puny, ailing

drint *v* : to fade, as a dress

driv *v* : drove

drop by *n* : casual visit

drop one's goodies *v* : made a mistake

drop-in *n* : a casual visitor, transient

drop-dumpling *n* : dumpling of corn meal

drotted, dratted, drattet *interj* : oath for <God rotted.>

drown the miller *v* : pour too much water into the spirits when mixing grog

drudge *v* : dredge, as in <to ~ oysters.>

drunkards *n* : small flies that fly about and light in sweetened liquors

drunk as a fiddler's bitch *phr* : very drunk

druthers *n* : desires <If I had my ~, I'd be a happy man.>

dry drizzle *n* : a sprinkle of rain, a light shower

dry grin *n* : embarrassed smile

to have the dry-grins *phr* : teased but striving to smile

dry month *n* : a farm hand hired by the dry month receives a month's wages after 24 days of work. He gets no pay for days too wet to work in the fields

dry out *n* : to melt down fat, to render lard by cooking animal flesh

dry wilts *n* : a condition of extreme decrepitude or desiccation

duberous *adj* : dubious, doubtful

duckins' *n* : everyday clothes, usually overalls

dudab, dudad *n* : a frill, fussy ornament

dudgeon *n* : resentment, sullen rage

duftail *n* : dovetail

dumb bull *n* : a kind of drum, hollow log with raw hide stretched over one end

dumb brute *n* : any domestic animal

dumb-cake *n* : cake made in silence on St. Mark's Eve, with numerous ceremonies, by girls, to discover their future husbands

dumb chill *n* : chill accompanied by shaking

dumperling *n* : dumpling

dung out *v* : to clean, to carry out rubbish

durgen *n* : an awkward, uncouth hillsman

dusk-dark, dusty-dark *n* : dusk

dust *v* : to move rapidly, as at a square dance

duster *n* : shaker, like a salt or pepper shaker

duster *n* : sandstorm

Dutchman's razor *n* : when a person treads in dung, he is said to have cut his foot with a Dutchman's razor

dutt *n* : dirt

duty-girl *n* : servant

- E -

each *n* : itch

easin' powder *n* : medicine that eases pain

east *n* : yeast

Easter flower *n* : forsythia

eat a bite *v* : have lunch

eater *n* : a fruit that can be eaten out of hand

eaves trough *n* : gutter

edify *v* : to educate

edzact *adj* : exact

eegit *n* : idiot

eench *n* : inch

egg-bread *n* : cornbread made with an egg

egg on *v* : to dare, encourage someone to do something

eke *n* : material added to a dress pattern

ell *n* : 45-inch yard

ellenyard *n* : a yardstick

ellum *n* : elm

elst *n* : else

embrangled *v* : entangled

emmet *n* : a very black ant

end-irons *n* : andirons

endurable *adj* : durable

enduring 1: *prep* during <I'll be back ~ the week.> **2:** *adj* entire <They stayed the ~ day.>

enjoy *v* : to entertain <We tried to ~ them.>

enough to choke a horse *phr* : plenty to eat

enurf *adv* : enough

epitap *n* : epitaph

error *n* : arrow

essoin *n* : excuse for not appearing in court on time

even-down *adj* : downright, bold-faced <She just told me an ~ lie.>

ever *adj* : every

everly *adv* : continually, at all times

ever'thing *n* : everything

everwhat *n* : whatever

everwhich *phr* : whichever <He threw the ball ~ way.>

everything an' all *phr* : a phrase expressing completeness, the entire

evils *n* : evil spirits, goblins

ewst *v* : used <He ~ to go.>

excussion *n* : excursion

extrornary *adj* : extraordinary

eye scraim *n* : ice cream

eye scraim

eye-stone, eye seed *n* : small object used to remove foreign bodies from the eye

- F -

fack *n* : fact

fadey *adv* : faded

faddle *n* : nonsense

faints *n* : fence

fainty *adj* : faint, feeble, languid, exhausted

fair off *v* : become clear, less cloudy

fair up *v* : to clear off, bright, clear off; to become clear or less cloudy

fall *v* : chop down, usually a tree

fallacy *n* : fault <It was my ~.>

falling table *n* : table with leaves that let down

fall out with *v* : argue

family woman *n* : a pregnant woman

fantods *n* : fit of the sulks, fidgets

fan-foot 1: *n* a woman who brazenly courts men's favors **2:** *v* to court

far *n* or *v* : fire

farce *v* : to stuff a fowl

farm liquor *n* : ordinary homespun whiskey —*Var* field whiskey

farting spell *n* : a short space of time

fascinator *n* : woman's crocheted head scarf

fasset *n* : faucet

fasting spittle *n* : the saliva of a fasting person, formerly held very effective in ceremonies, charms, also used in a remedy

fastly *adv* : firmly

fatty bread *n* : bread with cracklings in it

fault *v* : blame <Nobody can ~ you.>

faultin' *v* : to blame

faut *n* : fault

favor 1: *n* fever **2:** *v* to spare a part of the body **3:** *v* to resemble someone

favorance *n* : resemblance

fawmin *n* : farming

fawnch *v* : to clamor, raise a disturbance

fearder *adv* : more afraid

feather into *v* : to shoot

feder *n* : feather

feech *n* : finch (the bird)

feel on the bum *phr* : feel worthless

feels *n* : fields

feeze *v* : worry, fret

feist *v* : to behave coquettishly or provocatively

fence lifter *n* : heavy rain

ferm *n* : fern

ferninst *adj* : opposite to, against

fer piece *n* : a distance, a long way

ferro *n* : insect, locust

fer why *adj* : for why

fetch *v* : to bring, go

few bit *adj* : rather, a little

fibs *n* : the number five when counting marbles; as in dubs, thribs, fourses, fibs

fice *n* : a small, worthless dog

fiddler *n* : a small mottled or spotted catfish, also a young channel catfish

field whiskey *n* : homemade whiskey

fillum *n* : film

find, found *v* : to bear a child <I'm agoin' to ~ a baby afore long.>

fine-haired *adj* : inclined to put on airs, see also airyfied

finickin *adj* : fussy, fastidious

fire and fall back *phr* : drink and make room for others at the bar

fireboard *n* : mantel

fired or farred *n* : forehead

fire dogs *n* : andirons (See also dog irons)

fire-fanged *v* : dried up as if by fire <That corn is so brown it looks like it has been ~.>

fire fishing *n* : spearing or gigging fish at night with burning pine knots for illumination

fire hunting *n* : deer hunting at night with a torch

first light *n* : dawn

fisgig **1:** *n* worthless fellow **2:** *n* a light-hearted wench **3:** *adj* frisky

fish fry *n* : social gathering, usually a church or community picnic at which fish are served

fish muddle *n* : fish stew; also a gathering where it is eaten (but not a fish fry)

fissgig *n* : fish-gig, a spear used in catching fish

fist *v* : to beat with fists

fistes *n* : fists

fist holler *n* : mythical place where arguments are settled by fisticuffs

fit *v* : fought

fitten *n* : fit <It ain't ~.>

fit to kill *phr* : dressed up

fittyfied *adj* : subject to fits —*Var* fitified

fix *v* : prepare a meal

fix his wagon *v* : get revenge, get even <I'm gonna ~.>

fixin' *v* : preparing

flair *n* : flower

flang *v* : fling or flung

flannel cake *n* : pancake

flannen *n* : flannel

flapdoodle *n* : food for fools

flat 'backer *n* : plug tobacco

flatform *n* : platform

flat out *adv* : for certain

flaw *n* : a sudden gust of wind

flawy *adj* : subject to sudden gusts of wind

flea *v* : to skin

fleak-fat *n* : flake fat; large flakes of fat on a hog's belly

fleed *v* : flayed, skinned

fleek *v* : to come out

flinders *n* : splinters

flint buster *n* : mountaineer, hillbilly

flint rock *n* : piece of flint

flitter *v* : fritter

flitter *n* : female genitals

flitters *n* : pieces, rags, tatters

Florida-flip *n* : two-handed card game, popular with Southern blacks

flosh *v* : to spill, shake over

flour bread *n* : bread made from wheat rolled flat and cut into four- to five-inch squares

flow *n* : floor

flowit *v* : stomp on the gas pedal

flummux *v* : to perplex, embarrass, bewilder, defeat

flummixed *adj* : excited, bewildered

flusteration *n* : state of being flustered, confused

flustrate *v* : to fluster

flying Dutchman *n* : primitive, homemade merry-go-round, also a flying jenny

flying jenny *n* : a merry-go-round, usually homemade

flying-seal *n* : an unsealed letter

fly off the handle *phr* : lose one's temper

to fly the handle *v* : to give up quickly

fly-up-the-creek *n* : a giddy, capricious person

foam *n* : phone

fob *v* : to pocket

fode *n or v* : ford

foe *n* : four

Fo' Gawd, Fo' God *interj* : Before God! Oath usually precedes an observation

foil *v* : file

fool *adj* : full, as in <a ~ stomach.>

fool's fumbling ball *n* : joking, teasing, even sarcastic answer to what one may consider a stupid question, an evasive answer

fool up *v* : full

footback *n* : on foot

foot-pie *n* : apple turnover

foot washing *n* : a religious ceremony

for certain *adv* : certainly

forebay *n* : end of sluice where water meets the mill wheel

forestick *n* : front log in fireplace

forgainst *prep* : against <It's over ~ the mountain.>

forid *adj :* forward, impudent

forment, fornenst *prep* : against, opposite

fornet *n* : even, along the side of <We got ~ the other car.>

forrud *adv* : forward

for sure *adv* : certainly

forty ways from Sunday *phr* : going off in all directions

fossicate *v* : suffer from extreme heat, lack of air, suffocate

fotch, fotcht *v* : fetch, bring

fotch-on *adj* : imported, not locally grown or produced

found *v* : fined <The judge ~ him $10.>

founder *v* : to overfeed, overeat

foutham *v* : to fathom

fox *v* : to intoxicate, fuddle

fox-head *n* : moonshine whiskey

foxy *n* : drunk

fraction *n* : friction

fraid hole *n* : cyclone cellar

frail 1: *n* flail, an implement for beating grain **2:** *v* whip a child

fram *v* : strike a child with a book

fransy *n* : madness, near madness

frazzle *n* : very small amount, in weight

freality *n* : liberality

freemartin *n* : cow-calf twin of a bull-calf and thought always to be barren

French harp *n* : harmonica

Frenchmen *n* : tall spindly tobacco plants of useless quality

freshing *adv* : raining hard

fresh married *phr* : recently married

frill *n* : piece of fat on a hog's entrails

fritter-minded *adj* : frivolous, erratic

friz *v* : froze, also frozen

frog *n* : any toad or frog

frog-spit *n* : the froth that surrounds mayfly eggs that hatch in the spring

frog sticker *n* : pocket knife with a long, pointed blade

frogstool *n* : toadstool

frog storm *n* : period of bad weather in the spring, following several warm clear days

frog strangler *n* : heavy downpour

frolic *n* : a dance, a party

frolicate *v* : to have fun at a dance

from can to cain't *phr* : sunup to sundown

from stem to gudgeon *phr* : completely, entirely

frosses, frostes *n* : frosts

fruit *v* : to result in, to produce an effect

fruit jar *n* : glass jar for canning fruit or vegetables

fruit jar sucker *n* : hillbilly

frush *adj* : fresh

fuddle *v* : to make drunk

fuddle-britches *n* : wise-cracker, smart aleck

full-butt *n* : point blank with full force

fum *prep* : from

funeralize *v* : to hold a funeral or memorial service

funky *adj* : having a bad spell

funning *v* : joking

fur *n* : furrow

furmety *n* : wheat boiled in milk and seasoned

fur piece, fur pace, far piece *n* : some distance away

furriner *n* : stranger

fuss *n* : first

fuss and feathers *phr* : lot of talk, little action

fustrate *n* : first rate

fuzzed up *v* : disturbed, excited

- G -

gal *v* : to go looking for women

gal boy *n* : an effiminate boy

in the gales *phr* : cheerful, in good humor, even hilarious

gallery *n* : a porch

galloping fence *n* : a rail fence

gallows *adj* : reckless, dashing, showy

gallowses, galluses *adj* : ornery <He belongs to a ~ crowd.>

gallus *n* : suspenders

gallwances *n* : chick peas

gallynipper *n* : gigantic mosquito; any large flying insect that looks like a mosquito

gally-wampus *n* : an amphibious monster

galoopus *n* : a fabulous bird, like a great black eagle, said to lay square eggs

gambaters *n* : gambadoes, pranks or escapades

gambling stick *n* : gambrel, a stick used to insert in the hind legs of a slaughtered hog to hang it up

game *adj* : lame

gammon *n* **1:** idle talk, untruths **2:** bacon, sidemeat

gammoner *n* : a talkative, unreliable person

ganging *v* : walking

gansey *n* : a knitted, woolen shirt

gap *n* : gate

gaps *n* : disease of young chickens

garb-out *v* : to dress, or over-dress

gar-broth *n* : a broth made from a gar, a lowly regarded fish, thus usually applied derogatorily

garden-house *n* : a privy, outdoor toilet

gardeen *n* : guardian

garden peas *n* : green peas

garden sass *n* : vegetables from the garden

gardien *n* : guardian

gashly *adj* : ghastly, pale

gate *v* : get

gather *v* : to pick

gather, gathered *v* : bite <A snake ~ him by the ankle.>

gathering *n* : a boil or abscess; a festering

gator-sweat *n* : liquor buried in the ground for about five years

gaum, gorm *n* : mess, muddle, a poor job

gaum, gaumed *v* : to soil, smear <The players got their suits ~ up.>

gawk, gowk *n* : snipe-hunting <He's gone hunting the ~.>

gaysome *adj* : happy

gearp *v* : to stretch open

gears *n* : harness

gearth *n* : girth

gee *v* **1:** to agree, suit, fit; get along together **2:** to move to one side

geechy *n* : Low country term for Negro; originally <Ogeechee> as in the Ogeechee River in Georgia where slaves were landed

geechy mess *n* : food prepared from old-fashioned methods

geemany *n* : a mild oath

geenavy *n* : large number

gee-whollicker 1: *n* a wonder, marvel, something amazingly fine **2:** *adj* large or otherwise surprising

gen, gin *prep* : after, when, if

gentleman *n* : a category of Southern men usually distinguishable by their manners and not necessarily their wealth

Georgia buggy *n* : a wheelbarrow

Georgia ice cream *n* : grits

Georgia skin game *n* : a card game

gess *n* : guest

gether *v* : to gather

get high behind *v* : hurry

get his goat *v* : to annoy someone

get out of the wrong side of the bed *phr* : get up grumpy

get shut of *v* : get rid of something or someone

get wind of *v* : first to learn something not announced

Giasticutus *n* : legendary bird of prey with 50-foot wingspan which carries off full-grown cattle

gib *v* : to gut fish

giggle-soup *n* : homemade alcoholic beverage

gig lamps *n* : spectacles

gig lamps

gimber-jawed *adj* : protruding lower jaw —*Var* jimmy-jawed

gin *v* : given

gin *adv* : when, as soon as

gin *prep* : before, by the time that

ginning *v* : beginning

ginnin' around *v* : to move about

gipsen snow *n* : light snow

giste *n* : a joist

git *v* : get

git-flip *n* : guitar —*Var* pick-fiddle

git shet of *v* : get rid of

gittin' *n* : a load, a lot, a help-ing of food

gittin' along *v* : getting along

give down *v* : to admit, con-fess

give it a lick *v* : try some-thing different

give off *v* : to pretend

give-out **1:** *n* an announce-ment **2:** *adj* exhausted <I'm 'bout ~.>

givey, givy *adj* **1:** unsteady **2:** moist or soft <The weath-er is a little ~ this morning.>

gizzard-shad *n* : alewives

glade-kid *v* : to exaggerate

glair *n* : the white of an egg

gleam *v* : to glean

glebe *n* : turf, soil, farming land

glister *n* : an injection in the rectum

glut *n* : a wooden wedge used in splitting logs

glut shoes *n* : homemade shoes, made on a last that looks like a glut, usually fits either foot

ghosties *n* : ghosts

gnabble *v* : to nibble

gnat ball *n* : dense swarm of gnats or other insects

to a gnat's heel *phr* : exact or precise

go-devil *n* **1:** mole cricket **2:** a heavy wedge as used to split logs

go-down *adj* : sickly

goggle *v* : gargle

go halvers *v* : share equally

going to hell in a hand bas-ket *phr* : things are going badly

going with *v* : going steady

gollop **1:** *n* a large morsel **2:** *v* to swallow greedily

gollywog *n* : mythical mon-ster, like a giant salamander

gone gosling *n* **1:** a doomed person, animal, or thing **2:** a person hopelessly in difficul-ties **3:** a dead person

goobers, goober peas *n* : peanuts

gooch *v* : to dig or poke <Don't ~ me in the ribs.>

goochy *adj* : goosey, ticklish

Good-man *n* : God

in good heart *phr* : feeling well, in good spirits

good many *n* : a lot, quite a few

good old boy *n* : Southern male who is in control and in the know

good size *adj* : large

goody *n* : toothsome, especially sweet food, such as jelly, butter <I ain't got no ~ on my bread.>

goomer *v* : to bewitch

goomer doctor *n* : a witch doctor

goose *v* : to weed, using geese

goose drownder *n* : a cloudburst, very heavy rain

goozle, gozzle *n* **1:** guzzle **2:** the throat <I got a sore ~.>

gopher *n* : primitive plow

gorm *n* **1:** *n* a mess, all sticky **2:** *v* to smear, as with anything sticky

gormandize *v* : to eat in a greedy way

gormandizer *n* : a glutton

gormy *adj* : smeary, sticky

gorn *adj* : dirty, from oil and dirt usually

goslins *n* : said of a young boy whose voice has just changed <He has the ~.>

gospel-bird *n* : chicken, also a gospel fowl; traditionally served fried for Sunday's midday meal

goss *n* : an unnamed punishment

go to grass *phr* : friendly rebuke, among children

go-to-hell collar *n* : wing collar worn by men in formal dress

go to the bridge with him *v* : to befriend, support, stand by

go to the brush *v* : use the toilet

go to the well *phr* : an expression of loyalty

gound *n* : gown

gourdy *adj* **1:** green, green as a gourd **2:** countrified, unsophisticated

gouts *n* : lumps of clotted blood

government socks *n* : no socks at all, bare feet

gown, gawn *v* : gone

gowrow *n* : a fabulous reptile, an enormous man-eating lizard

grabble *v* **1:** to dig potatoes out of a hill, leaving the plant **2:** to dig out of the ground with hands

gracious *n* : large amount, lot of

gracious plenty *n* : more than enough

grain *adj* : a little, a small amount <He's a ~ sickly.>

grains *n* : greens

gramy *v* : to vex, upset

grand-rascal *n* : a cheat, con man

granny, granny-woman *n* : midwife, grandmother

grannycat *n* : small square-nosed yellow catfish

grass-gall *n* : sore between the toes of people who walk barefoot in the summer, supposedly caused by the dew

grass sack *n* : burlap bag

grass-widow *n* **1:** a woman separated temporarily from her husband **2:** unmarried person with a child

grave *v* : to clean a ship's bottom by burning or scraping off seaweed, barnacles and putting on more pitch

gravel *v* : to embarrass, humiliate

graveyard cough *n* : deep, hollow cough

graveyard widow *n* : woman whose husband has died

gray-mare *n* : a wife who rules her husband

graze *v* : grease

grease light *n* : crude lamp made of a saucer or shell filled with lard and using a rag wick —*Var* slut, or slut lamp

great big *adj* : large

great shakes *n* : thing of great account; usually used in the negative <She cooked supper but it was no ~.>

greedy gut *n* : a glutton

green *v* : to ridicule, to tease, make the butt of a joke

greens *n* : cooked salad greens

greenup *n* : springtime

grigri *n* : a charm, to cast a spell

ground *v* : grind <It will take all day to ~ the corn.>

grindlestone *n* : a grind stone

grinning like a mule eating briars *phr* : a wide grin

grine *n* : groin

gripes *n* **1:** grapes **2:** a stomach or intestinal disorder

gripey *adj* : causing sharp bowel pain

grissle *n* : gristle

gritter *n* : grater, usually for corn

grog blossom *n* : nose inflammation from excessive drinking

gross-bump *n* : pimples on youth

ground itch *n* : athlete's foot, other rashes attributed to the toxic action of dew on the bare skin; also called dew poison

ground peas *n* : peanuts

ground rations *n* : sexual intercourse

grouty *adj* : sulky or surly

grow like Topsy *phr* : sudden growth in a child

grub hyson *n* : sassafras tea

grum *adj* : glum

grumble guts *n* : a confirmed grumbler

grumtion *adj* : scrumptious

grun-sill *n* : ground-sill, timber of a structure next to ground

grutch *v* : begrudge

guan'ner *n* : guano

guano sack, gunny sack *n* : burlap bag

guff *n* : gulf

guffins *n* : very large feet

guggle *v* : to gurgle

guinea-keet *n* : guinea fowl

gulf *n* : golf

gull *n* **1:** girl **2:** a simpleton, one easily cheated

gull around *v* : to court, follow

Gullah *n* : dialect spoken by blacks along coastal areas of South Carolina and Georgia

gulluck *n* : gullet

gullup *n* : the amount of liquid that can be poured from a jug or bottle before the container gets air

gully-washer *n* : thunderstorm, heavy rain

guma *n* : seminal fluid

gumbo *n* : a tough, hard clay soil

gum crib *n* : crib fashioned from a hollow log

gumption *n* : ambition

gum wadding *n* : disparaging term for bread, usually bread that didn't rise

gut 1: *v* got **2:** *n* an arm of a creek, in saltwater

guttler *n* : a glutton

gwine *v* : going

gyarden *n* : garden

gyp *n* : female dog

- H -

haath *n* : hearth

hab *v* : have

hack *n* : under control by others <She's got him under ~.>

had it *v* : fed up

had it in for *v* : a grudge <He's ~ me ever since I broke his mower.>

hadn't ought *v* : shouldn't

haggly *v* : hacked unevenly

hail *n* : hell

hail-salt *n* : coarse salt

hail-shot *n* : small shot for cannon, grape shot

haint *n* : ghost

hair, haired *v* : to inherit <He ~ his pap's land.>

hair *adv* : here

half-ham *n* : a hop, skip, and a jump

half-head bedstead *n* : bed with bed posts shorter than the headboard

half-sole yourself *v* : to refill your glass when it is only half empty

half-strainer *n* : social climber

Hall's dog *n* : inclined to idleness <He's lazy as ~.>

halo *interj* : hello

ham *pron* : him

hambrow *n* : coarse sheets made of flax

hampered *v* : jailed

handily *adv* : readily, justly <You can't ~ blame a man.>

handkercheer *n* : handkerchief

hankyhead *n* : person who wears a handkerchief knotted at the four corners as a cap

handle talk *v* : to gossip

handpocket *n* : bag, handbag

hand-running *adv* : continuously

hand-speak *n* : pole six to eight feet long used in logging and at log rolls

hand's-turn *n* : a piece of work of any kind

hangman's choice *n* : choice between two evils

hant *n* : haunt, ghost

happen *v* : to suffer, receive <He ~ to a right bad hurt.>

happen-so *n* : an accident, a fluke

happy *n* : a toy <He give the baby his ~.>

har *n* : hair

harbour *v* : to frequent

hard *v* : hired

hard ague *n* : severe chill

hard-got *n* : obtained with difficulty

hardness *n* : bitterness between people, neighbors

in a hard row of stumps *phr* : in a bad way, usually in financial straits

hard row to hoe *n* : a difficult undertaking

hardshell Baptist *n* : strict Baptist

hash *v* : to finish or make an end to opposition

hast *v* : has

hate *n* : hat

hate, hait *n* : bit, small amount <I don't care a ~.>

hatrack *n* : an old cow

haul ass *v* : hurry off

havance *n* : good manners, behavior

have off *v* : take off

have sand in one's gizzard *phr* : courageous <He has sand in his gizzard.>

have the wrong end of the poker *phr* : be on the losing side, a bad bargain

havvers *n* : claiming half of whatever another finds

hawk *v* : to exasperate, to chagrin

hawse *n* : horse

hay cock *n* : pile of hay, also hay doodle

hayem *n* : ham

hay shacker *n* : country bumpkin

hayshant *n* : rascal, an annoying child

hazel splitter *n* : a wild, lean hog, a razorback

head *n* **1:** in mind **2:** a copperhead snake

head cap *n* : platform on small boat, at the bow

headest start *n* : an advantage

heading *n* : a pillow

heah *adv* : here

heap *adv* : much

heap sight *n* : a lot <I'd ~ rather let him take the mower back than get him riled again.>

hearing *n* : a written reply to a letter

hearn *v* : heard <I ~ you say something ugly.>

heart in one's pocket *phr* : to become indifferent toward a woman whom one has been courting

heating stone *n* : metal heater

hector *v* : to treat with insolence, bully

heel *n* : large amount

heel it *v* : to walk rapidly

he-kicking *adj* : alive, fresh

hell *n* : hill

hell fire *interj* : exclamation of jubilance or frustration. —*Var* hell's bell's, hell's fuzzy

hellum *n* : helm

hem *n* : ham

hen-flint *n* : chicken dung

hen-wood *n* : chittamwood, also called buckthorn or smoke tree, used sometimes for knife handles

hep *n* or *v* : help

herby *adj* : having the flavor of herbs

hern *pron* : hers

herrin-gutted *adj* : thin, poor, lean

herring *n* : hearing

hessian *n* : a term of reproach, usually applied to a vicious or meddlesome old woman

hickey *n* : sea-saw, also a boil

hickory *n* **1:** a switch **2:** a rapid gait

hickory-limb oil *n* : a whipping <His teacher was administering a dose of ~.>

hickory-shad *n* : gizzard shad, a variety of fish that spawns in rivers in the early spring

hide nor hair *phr* : not in view <I ain't seen ~ of him.>

high-behind *n* **1:** a mythical lizard as big as a bull **2:** a bloodthirsty enemy to all mankind

higher than a Georgia pine *phr* : very drunk

high-headed *adj* : proud, arrogant, spirited

high-heel time *n* : good times

high Henry *n* : a railroad train

high-lonesome *n* : debauch, spree

high-minded *adj* : arrogant, proud

high on the hog *phr* : well off <They been living ~ lately.>

high pockets *n* : a tall person

high sheriff *n* : the elected sheriff

high sign *v* : signal

high time *adv* : overdue <It's ~ you took that mower back.>

hiket *v* : leave

hillbilly *n* : a very rural mountain dweller —*Var* flint buster, acorn-cracker, briar hopper, bush buster, brush ape, elmer, ellum-peeler, fruit jar sucker, haw-eater, hay shacker, hog ranger, puddle jumper, pumpkin roller, rabbit-twister, ridge-runner, sorghum lapper, sprout straddler, squirrel-turner, 'tatergrabber, weed bender

hindside first *adv* : backwards

hind-sights *n* : the Old Testament

hippin's *n* : diapers

hippoed *adj* : suffering from an imaginary ailment <That poor ~ old woman.>

hip-shot *adj* : lame, awkward

hip-swinney *n* : a weakness of the back

hired out *v* : working for someone else

hiring day *n* : scheduled court day before Christmas, when landowners hired field hands and other servants for the next year

hisn *pron* : his

hisself *pron* : himself

hissy *n* : fit of anger

histe *v* : hoist

hit *pron* : it

hobbledehoy *n* : youth, especially awkward youth

hockey *n* or *v* : child's word for feces, defecate

hockset *n* : hogshead

hoe *n* : a frying pan

hoe cake *n* : cornbread of meal and water fried on a griddle

hog *n* : hug <He gave her a ~ and a kiss.>

hog down corn *n* : to turn hogs into a field and allow them to eat what's left

hog jowl and blackeyed peas *n* : a combination eaten on New Year's Day for good luck

hog-killin' *n* : any sort of hilarious celebration

hog-killin' time *n* **1:** a cold snap **2:** a highly enjoyable time

hog-leg *n* : a large pistol or revolver

hogmolly *n* : a fish, a spotted sucker

hog ranger *n* : farm rube

hog slops *n* : slops fed to hogs

since the hogs et grandma (or little brother) *phr* : expression of great amusement <I ain't had so much fun ~.>

hoigh, hoy *adj* : high

hold his feet to the fire *phr* : force an issue

hold onto your hat *phr* : surprising news <~ because you ain't gonna believe this.>

hold your horses *phr* : calm down

hold your potato *v* : to be patient

hole *n* : hall <He got his license down at city ~.>

holler *n or v* : yell, scream

holler calf-rope *v* : to acknowledge defeat

Holly Eve *n* : Halloween

holpen *v* : helped

holt *v* : hold

hominy *phr* : how many

hone 1: *n* horn **2:** *v* to yearn, long for

hone for *v* : to long for, to desire strongly, crave

honeyfuggle *v* : to cajole, wheedle

honor *v* : to bow, a term used in square dancing, as <~ your partner.>

hook *n* : signature

hoorah *v* : to make haste, to hurry

hooter *n* : a drink <Let's go over to the bar for a ~>

Hoover gravy *n* : gravy of flour and water and other condiments

Hoover ham *n* : salt pork; term used in the Depression during the Hoover administration

Hoover pork *n* : rabbit meat; term used during the Depression

hoozle, hoot *n* : drink of liquor

hop *n* : harp

hope *v* : help

hope *n* : an inlet

hoppergrass

hoppergrass *n* : grasshopper

hopper-tailed *adj* : having broad or prominent buttocks, usually applied to men

hopping mad *adj* : very angry

hoppin' john *n* : dish of black-eyed peas cooked with hog jowl, usually eaten on New Year's Day for good luck

horde *adv* : hard

horn *n* : a measure of liquid

horny *adj* : amorous

horse dose *n* : a very large dose of medicine

horse-in *n* : a marble game

horse quart *n* : a large size

hot *n* : heart

hot as blue blazes *phr* : very hot

hot damn *interj* : an exclamation of happiness

hot-do *n* : extravagant act, outlandish thing

hot pepper *n* : a kind of ball game

hotten *v* : to heat

houms *n* : mudflats or swampy places that dry up in summer

hour by sun *n* : time stated with relation to rising or setting sun

house *n* : a living room, sitting room

house-plunder *n* : household furniture, furnishings

house servants *n* : servants who work only in the house, contrasted with yardmen and field hands who work outside

how come *phr* : how something happens, usually a question

how-do piece *n* : visor of a cap

howell *n* : a cooper's tool for smoothing barrel staves

hrup *v* : whip, to whip

hudder *n* : cap on a stack of wheat

hull *n* : shotgun shell, a spent shell

hull-gull *n* : a guessing game played with pebbles or other small objects; sometimes called a hully-gully

hum *n* : home

hunker *n* : haunches

hunker down *v* : to squat

hunky dory *adj* : everything is okay

hurang *n* : household rumpus among children

huroosh *n* : noise, rush

hurrah *v* : hurry

hurt *n* : heart

hurty *adv* : causing pain <These ~ shoes are killing me.>

hush-mouth *adj* : close-lipped

hush-puppy *n* : patty of corn-bread

hush your mouth *phr* : shut up!

huslement *n* : furniture, odds and ends

huss *n* **1:** hell **2:** husk

hut *n* : hurt

– I –

ice cool *n* : high school

I declare *phr* : exclamation said to let the talker know you are listening

I do believe *phr* : usually a prelude to giving an opinion

idlesome *adj* : given over to idleness and sloth

idy *n* : idea

iffy *adj* : uncertain

if that don't beat all *phr* : an exclamation of surprise

ile *n* : oil

ill *adj* : angry, evil tempered

I'll be doggone *phr* : an exclamation of wonder

ill-conditioned *adj* : ill-tempered

ill-convenient *adj* : inconvenient

I'm here to tell you *phr* : said for emphasis <~ that wasn't the way it was.>

in a bad way *phr* : seriously ill <She's laid up and ~.>

in a family way *adj* : pregnant

in and about *adv* : approximately

in a swivet *phr* : nervous haste

Indian hen *n* : the pileated woodpecker

Indian pone *n* : cake made of flour or meal, like biscuit, sometimes with eggs

infare *n* **1:** celebration on the day following a wedding, at home of groom's parents; sometimes a reception by the groom's parents for the bride and groom **2:** a dinner given on the day of the wedding

ingun *n* : onion

inkle *v* : attend a party without invitation

instrument *n* : penis

in this day and time *adv* : now

intment *n* : ointment

intostication *n* : intoxication

i'on *n* : iron

iron *v* : earn

islants *n* : islands

istocrats *n* : derived from aristocrats, used in contempt

itchies *n* : winter clothing

itsy-bitsy *adj* : small

ixperance *n* : experience

izzard *n* : letter Z <He can say the alphabet from A to ~.>

- J -

jackleg *n* : a semi-skilled artisan

jacksalmon *n* : the walleyed pike

jaggedy *adj* : jagged

jags *n* : tatters, as in <rags and ~.>

jakeleg *adv* : condition of walking after drinking bad liquor

jakes *n* : a privy

jakey *adj* : countrified, old-fashioned, uncouth

jambalaya *n* **1:** a mixture of rice and ham **2:** potpourri

jam-up *adj* : first rate, dependable

janders *n* : jaundice

ja'nt *n* : jaunt

jape *v* : cohabit

jaw *v* : to talk

jaybird *n* : without clothes <He was naked as a ~.>

Jeams *n* : James

jedge *n* : judge

jell *n* : jail

Jenewary *n* : January

jenny *n* : a man busied with women's affairs

jerp *n* : a small amount, usually of sweets

Jesse *v* : to give a scolding

jess-ellif *n* : a fish found in the Ozarks, also known as the hog-sucker or hogmolly. The name was originally applied in derision of a man named Ellif who was supposed to resemble the fish

jew *n* or *adj* : dew, due

jibble *v* : to cut into small pieces

jib-rags *n* : strips or small pieces of rags

jice *n* : joist

jiggamy *n* : an implement or tool

jiggerate *v* : to function or operate

jiggumbob *n* : something strange, peculiar, or unknown

jillikens *n* : backwoods

jim **1:** *n* jam **2:** *v* to damage, mar, deface

jimber-jawed, jimmy-jawed *n* or *adj* : projecting lower jaw

jimjams *n* : delirium tremens

jim-kay *v* : to stuff with food

jimmy-john *n* : demijohn, a large glass bottle with a narrow neck and a wicker covering

jimplicute *n* : a ghostly dragon supposed to walk the roads at night

jimson-weed *n* : Jamestown weed, a poisonous weed of the nightshade family

jimswinger *n* : long-tailed coat of the Prince Albert style

jine *v* : join

jint *n* : joint, giant

jit *n* : a nickel

Job's comforter *n* : one who depresses and discourages under the appearance of consoling

Job's teeth *n* : hard beans on a string for teething

joe *v* : to move something slowly

joe-darter *n* : an unsurpassed person or thing

joe-sack *n* : a chemise

John Henry *n* **1:** a dude, a rustic Beau Brummel **2:** a penis in coastal Virginia and South Carolina

johnny-cake *n* : cornmeal cake, cornbread —*Var* journey cake, jannock, jonnock

joices *n* : joists

joint *n* : giant

joky fellow *n* : a clown, a mental defective, also a person with a lively disposition

jolt from Solomon's cradle *phr* : used to denote a lack of wisdom or intelligence

joree *v* : make fun of, jest

josey *n* : a little jacket

josie *n* : a woman's garment, something like a long undershirt

joskin *n* : a clownish fellow, a countryman

journey proud *v* : enthusiasm resulting from a trip <That trip to Paris sure made her ~.>

jower *v* : to argue, quarrel, wrangle

jowery *adj* : given to scolding, grumbling

jowerings *n* : scoldings

joy ride *n* : a short auto ride strictly for fun

juba *n* : a Negro dance

jubilo *n* : jubilee

judgematical *adj* : quizzical

juggles *n* : very large chips, usually of wood

to juice a cow *v* : to milk a cow

juke joint *n* : a beer hall with a jukebox

jularker *n* **1:** a type of bean **2:** boyfriend

juliper *n* : juice or gravy from cooked fowl or other meat

jump the broom 1: *v* to marry or propose marriage **2:** *n* an irregular marriage —*Var* jump over the broomstick

jump-up *n* : a meeting at which extemporaneous speeches are made

june *v* : to move briskly, to hurry

junk-bottle *n* : a black-gum bottle

jussel *v* : jostle

just as good *phr* : might just as well

juty *n* : duty

- K -

kain't *v* : can't
kain't hardly *v* : can't hardly
kain't help its *phr* : clumsiness <He's got a bad case of the ~.>
kapoodle *n* : group, crowd
katynipper *n* : dragonfly; see also gallynipper
kearb *n* : curb
kearbine *n* : carbine
keeler *n* : small wooden vessel
keen *v* : to wail, cry
keep close to the willows *v* : to be conventional, conservative, modest. Derives from nude boys who when swimming stayed close to the willows to avoid being seen naked
keep your dobbers up *v* : keep your courage up
keer *n* : care
keerful *adj* : careful
kerflip *adj* : fine, stylish, neat
ketchy *adj* : uncertain, unsettled, usually applied to weather

kettle-tea *n* : tea of hot water, milk, and sugar —*Var* cambric tea
kicked the traces *v* : took off
kill-devil *n* : high-proof whiskey of poor quality
kilt *v* : killed
kinry, kinnery *n* : kindred
kin *n* : family, no matter how distant
kin *v* : can
kindly *adv* : kind of <It's ~ chill today.>
king bee *n* : top person in group or organization
king's evil *n* : scrofula, swelling of the neck glands
kink *n* : an unreasonable or obstinate notion
kink over *v* : to fall over, faint
kitchen physic *n* : nourishing diet for a patient; good living
kitchen safe *n* : cupboard
kitchen-sweat *n* : a country dance
kitney *n* : kidney
kitt *n* : a small violin with three strings
kittle *n* : kettle
kittle an' bilin' *n* : the whole number, the entire group —*Var* kit and bile
kitty-corner *adv* : diagonally

kiver *n* : bed cover
kiyoodle *v* : to sing joyously
kiyutle *n* : a small dog
knackers *n* : testicles
knee-baby *n* **1:** walking
  baby **2:** a second child
knee high to a grasshopper
  phr : small, used to describe
  an infant
knock up *v* : make pregnant
knock around *v* : be idle
knowance, knowings *n* :
  knowledge <Hit ain't to my
  ~.>
knuckle puddin' *n* : beating
  with the fists
koosy *adj* : tacky, outmoded,
  in bad taste
kurl *v* : to hasten, run
kwarr *n* : choir

- L -

lace *v* : to beat, thrash
lack *adv* : like
lairs *n* : plenty
lally-gaggin **1:** *n* love-mak-
  ing; coquettish or flirtatious
  behavior **2:** *v* killing time
lamentate *v* : to lament, complain
lanch *v* : to lance
landloper *n* : vagabond,
  vagrant
land-poor *adj* : having a lot
  of land but unable to pay
  taxes on it
lane *n* : laying
lantern-jaws *n* : long thin
  jaws, thus a thin visage
lap *n* : treetop left on the
  ground after logging
lap-baby *n* : baby, infant old
  enough to sit in lap
laplander *n* : person who
  lives on the Missouri-
  Arkansas border
lapsided *adj* : lopsided
larapin *adj* : good, pleasing,
  delicious
lard-stand *n* : large can or jar
  of lard

lareover *n* : a ghost, mask, or skeleton to scare children

larker *n* : a mischievous fellow

larn *v* : learn

larp *n* : gravy

larrows *phr* : a joking, teasing, even sarcastic expression used to reply to someone without answering his question

larrup *v* : whip, flog, thrash

larruping *n* : a thrashing

larva *n* : a mask, usually to frighten children

laskins and lavins *n* : a great quantity

lasses *n* : molasses

last button on Gabe's coat *n* : the very last bit of anything, usually of bacon, whiskey, sugar, or other household commodities

lasty *adj* : lasting, durable

lat bub *n* : light bulb

latch string *n* : a string once used to open a door and hung out outside to let someone in; used as an expression of welcome

launch *n* : lunch

laurely *adj* : laurel covered

lavish *n :* abundance, plenty <They have a ~ of potatoes.>

law *v* : to enforce <They can't ~ me.>

law *n* : an officer of the law

lawdy mussy *interj* : Lord have mercy —*Var* lawsy mussy

lawk *n* : lock

lawn *adj* : long

lawrence *n* : a lazy moocher, a loafer, parasite

Lawzeeme *interj* : Lordie me, short for Lord save me

lax *n* : diarrhea

lay *v* : to bet <I ~ you catch it.>

lay back *v* : to save

lay by *v* : to plow the last time, to finish cultivation of, with plow, hoe

lay flats *n* : leaflets

laylock *n* : lilac

lay off *v* : plan, intend to do something

lay out *v* : to plan, to intend, also to be idle

layway *v* : to waylay, ambush

lay whippped *v* : to ride rapidly, to drive rapidly <We sure ~ it down the road.>

lazy boy *n* : scythe, sickle, for cutting weeds

lazy Tom *n* : a rude water mill for grinding corn

leaf *adv* : rather <I'd ~ do it.>

leaf *n* : permission, reward

learn *v* : teach

learned off *v* : become educated

least chap *n* : the youngest boy in the family

least one *n* : the youngest or smallest child

leather britches *n* : green beans dried and cooked in the pod

leave out of here *v* : to leave

leben *n* : eleven

leftment *n* : a fragment remaining

leg up *adj* : ahead of the rest

leg weary *adj* : tired of walking

less *v* : let us

less and leaster *adv* : smaller and smaller

lesson *conj* : unless

let loose *v* : fire at

let on *v* : to pretend

let out *v* : said when an activity ends <Church ~ on time on Sunday.>

letter *n* : spark on the wick of a burning candle, foretelling the coming of a letter

letter-mail *n* : a letter

level down *v* : drink, to cause level of fluid in a vessel to go down

lick *n* : a whack or blow

lick and a promise *phr* : temporary repairs, superficial treatment

lickety-whoop *adv* : at high speed

lick-log *n* : a fallen tree with big notches cut in it to hold salt for cattle

lick thumbs *v* : to reach an agreement

lickwish *n* : licorice

lick your flint *v* **1:** to prepare for a difficult talk **2:** to take precautions against disaster

lidard knot *n* : lightwood, wood that burns readily

lie a corpse *v* : to lie in state

lie bill *n* : a sworn statement

lie tale *n* : false and malicious story

liever *adv* : rather

lift *adj* : sick, or very weak

light a rag *v* : to depart suddenly, in a hurry

light a shuck *v* : to depart in haste

light bread *n* : ordinary bread made with yeast, also wheat bread, loaf bread

lighterd, light wood *n* : kindling, resinous pine wood

light into, lit into *v* : to attack verbally <He ~ the plumber about the bill.>

light out *v* : leave in a hurry

lightning bug revival *n* : summer-time tent revivals

lights *n* : lungs, innards

like to have *adv* : nearly, almost <I ~ split my britches I laughed so hard.>

lilting *v* : singing

lim *n* : limb

limb *v* : to whip, flog

limber-jack *n* **1:** person who moves his arms and legs in a very loose way **2:** a toy

limber-sick *adj* : weak, unable to stand or walk because of illness

limber-twig *n* : apple with long stem, hangs on the tree until frost

limby *adj* : having many limbs or branches

line *v* : to copulate, said of dogs

line-fishing *n* : fishing with a line

line-out *v* **1:** to organize **2:** to give out a hymn a line or two at a time to the singers

lines *n* : loins

line-tree *n* : a boundary-line tree

linimum *n* : liniment

lip *n* : back talk <Don't give me any more of your ~.>

liquish *n* : licorice.

liquorhead *n* : habitual drunkard

list *n* : ridge of earth thrown up by a plow, as in cultivating corn

listen at *v* : listen to

Litchet *n* : child's name for Richard

literary school *n* : the ordinary public school

litter *n* : letter

little house *n* : privy

little old *adj* : little, used familiarly

liver-pin *n* : figurative term to express the center or key part of the liver not clearly located <Damn his ~.>

live with the world *v* : to be concerned with worldly matters, material interests

living at the foot of the cross *phr* : religious conversion after a narrow escape from death

load *v* : to deceive with a windy or tall tale

loadened *v* : loaded

lobcock *n* : large woodpecker

lock *n* or *v* : lark, as in frolic

locusses *n* : locust trees

lodge *adj* : large

log-rollin' *n* **1:** a gathering of neighbors to roll logs on uncultivated land **2:** to roll logs to build a cabin

loin *v* : learn

lolliper *n* : something admirable or pleasing

lollop *v* : loll or lounge idly

long and merry ago *phr* : a long past, indefinite time <That happened ~.>

longbow *n* : to draw the long-bow means to exaggerate, tell improbable stories

long-corn *n* : longest and best earns of corn, used for bread

long-headed *adj* : shrewd, farseeing, discerning

long-home *n* : Heaven, house in Heaven

long-hundred *n* : one hundred and twenty

long johns *n* : long winter underwear

long-potatoes *n* : sweet potatoes

long-tongue *n* : a gossip

long-tongued *adj* : prating, babbling

looby *adj* : clumsy, awkward

look **1:** *n* a view from a slight eminence **2:** *v* lick <~ the stamp before puttin' it on the letter.>

look-a-here *v* : look here

look down on *v* : regard with disdain

loosenin' weed *n* : a purgative or laxative herb

lord *n* : lard

Lord sakes, Lord a mercy *interj* : exclamation denoting surprise

lose one's lunch *v* : to vomit

lost *n* : last

lost one's head *v* : lose one's temper

louse-path *n* : the part in one's hair

love-hole *n* : a gully or ditch across the road

love-lock *n* : separate lock of hair hanging conspicuously on the head

love-pain *n* : toothache

love-vine *n* : gold-thread

low-bush lightning *n* : hidden whiskey

low cotton *adj* : puny, state of depression

lowery *n* : threatening weather

low-lifed *adj* : lacking in respect, despicable

lown *n* : mild, balmy weather

low-rate *v* : to depreciate, downgrade

luck *v* : look <~ out, that tree is falling.>

luck out *v* : to have good luck in a venture

lucky-bone *n* : wishbone

lucky-bones *n* : two bony disks found in crawfish, thought to bring good luck

luggish *adj* : slow, heavy, sluggish

lumber *n* : loud noise

lumbered up *phr* : said of a room or yard overcrowded with furniture or implements

lumbering *n* : sound of distant thunder

lumbrage *n* : loud rumbling or crashing noise

lumping *adj* : bulky, chunky, heavy

lumpous *adj* : all in a heap

lunchbreak parsons *n* : part-time preachers

lunchy *adj* : hungry at lunch time

lust *adj* : lost

maddick *n* : mattock

mad-doctor *n* : doctor who treats the mentally disturbed

mad fence *n* : fence between adjoining farms

mad money *n* : money a girl takes on a date to get her home in case she gets mad with her escort

mad sow *n* : a sow in heat

maiden-land *n* : land acquired with a wife and lost upon her death

make *n* : a woman's figure

make a crop *v* : to farm a field

make a fancy *v* : make a good impression

make a habit *v* : to be habitual in something

make a mash *v* : get a crush on someone

make-do *n* : makeshift

make-game *n* : one who makes fun of another

make light *v* : to belittle

make no bones about it *v* : to have no pretense about something

make out like *v* : pretend

make over *v* : to show affection for

makes no never mind *phr* : it doesn't matter

make strange *v* : to be amazed or astonished

make the riffle *v* : to accomplish a given task

make tracks *v* : leave in haste

making down *v* : snowing hard

makvil *n* : marble

maladder *n* : mulatto

male brute *n* : male of domestic animals

mallyhack *v* : to cut up, to beat severely

malungeon, melungeon *n* : one of a race of people in Southwestern Virginia and eastern Tennessee said to have Indian blood; mixed race of eastern Tennessee and eastern North Carolina

mammock 1: *n* a shapeless piece, a fragment **2:** *v* to tear into pieces, mangle

manavel *v* : to pilfer eatables or articles of small value

manavellings *n* : odds and ends of food, scraps, small gratuities

mango call *n* : love call

maninose *n* : mannose, a soft clam

mannerable, mannersome *adj* : polite, having good manners

man's got to do what a man's got to do *phr* : Southern male expression to explain the unexplainable when it is a matter of honor

man-sworn *v* : to swear falsely

mantel shelf, mantel board *n* : mantel—*Var* fireboard

maple-head *n* : any man with a noticeably small head

marchantable *adv* : fit for sale

March flower *n* : daffodil

mare's nest *n* : an absurd or ridiculous imagined discovery

margent *n* : margin

marm *n* : form of ma'am, for madam

marr *n* : slush, shallow grassy pool in a swamp

marrow-bones *n* : knees, bones of the knees

marse *n* : master

marster *n* : master

martin storm *n* : a late blizzard

marvel *n* : marble

mash *n* : mesh, also a marsh

Mason-Dixon Line *n* :
boundary between Maryland
and Pennsylvania established
by the Missouri Compromise
of 1820 as the dividing line
between the free and slave
states

massacree *n* : massacre

mass dark *adv* : absolutely
dark

mast *n* **1:** acorns, nuts, col-
lectively **2:** food for animals

masterest *adv* : greatest

mater *n* : tomato

mater

mattery *adj* : purulent, gener-
ating pus

maul *v* : to split wood with
wedges and a heavy, usually
wooden, hammer

maws *n* : moss

may can, might could *v* :
may be able to

May-dew *n* : dew gathered on
a May morning and used to
wash the face, believed to be
a beautifier

May-hop *n* : the passion
flower vine

Maypop *n* : edible fruit of the
May-hop vine

meadow muffin *n* : cow dung

meal-bag *n* : bag which held
three bushels of corn

medlar *n* : meadow lark

meech, meach *v* : to slink, to
appear dishonest

meller *adj* : mellow

meller-bug *n* : mealy-bug

melt *n* : the spleen

mend his gait *v* : go faster

men-folks *n* : men, usually
referring to men of a family
or a group

meracle *n* : miracle

merrygold *n* : marigold

merrythought *n* : wishbone
of a fowl

mess *n* : a portion of, enough
for a meal <He's got a ~ of
greens.>

mess-ahead *adj* : shiftless,
improvident

methiglum *n* : fermented
drink made from honey

middle day *n* : noon

middle-man *n* : in a game of
marbles, the marble in the
center of the ring

middlin' 1: *adv* so so, about mid-way **2:** *adj* not in good health but not too sick either

middlin' meat *n* : bacon, sometimes salt pork

might could *v* : might

might near *adv* : nearly <It's ~ dark.>

mighty nice *adj* : especially nice

migrate *v* : to move, as from one room to another

milk-and-water *phr* : wishy-washy

mill clapper *n* : a constant talker

mill days *n* : days of moodiness, gloominess, and grouchiness

million *n* : melon

mimock *n* : one who mimics

mind, minded *v* : remind <He ~ me of my promise.>

ming-mang *n* : mixture of butter and molasses, sometimes butter and gravy

mine eyes *n* : mayonnaise

minister's face *n* : the upper part of the head of a hog

minnie, minner *n* : minnow

minniken *adj* : very small

minnum *n* : small fish

mint julep *n* : drink made with bourbon, sugar, water, mashed mint, and ice

miration *n* : surprise

miring time *n* : spring, when cattle are weak and thin and apt to get mired in soft marshes

miseries *n* **1:** pain from muscular or bone ailment, such as rheumatism, arthritis **2:** aches and pains **3:** any ailment <He's got the ~ today.>

misfool *v* : to delude, to deceive

mislick *n* : a false blow from an axe; false or awkward blow

mismeant *v* : past tense, to mistake

misput *v* : to mislay, misplace, lose

misremember *v* : to err by failing to remember

misseras *n* : Mrs.

Miss Nancy *n* : an effeminate young man

miss-woman *n* : a refined, accomplished young woman, either married or single

mitten *v* : jilt, to be rejected as a lover <She gave him the ~.>

mitten on *v* : to seize and hold on

mixtry *n* : mixture

Miz *n* : Mrs.

mizzle 1: *n* fine rain, light shower **2:** *v* to disappear suddenly

moaning *n* : morning

mobby *n* : liquor or juice pressed from apples or peaches to be used to distill brandy

mocker *n* : mockingbird

mockit *n* : market

moddity *n* : commodity

moil *v* : to be very painstaking

molasses mill *n* : machine for pressing liquid from cane

molewarp, moldwarp *n* : a senseless person

molly-hugging *n* : lovemaking

mollyjogger *n* : a kind of minnow

molosses *n* : molasses

mommick *n* : state of disorder

mommix *n* : a mess, a task badly done

mommocks *v* : to tease, annoy, torment

monack *n* : a woodchuck

monkey rum *n* : distilled syrup of sorghum cane

monsus *adv* : exceedingly, extremely, wonderfully <That's a ~ hard thing to do.>

moody *adj* : muddy

moon-calf *n* : a bastard, a simpleton

moon-eyed *adj* : dim-eyed, purblind

moonshine *n* : illegally made corn whiskey

moralize *v* : to make moral <It'll take a spell to ~ her.>

more than a farmer has hay *phr* : a great deal of something

morfadite *n* : hermaphrodite

morn gloam *n* : first light of morning

moron *adv* : more than

mort *n* : a quantity, a great number

mortases *n* : tomatoes

mosackle *n* : motorcycle

moss *n* : a lichen on the face of a rock

mossback *n* : an arch conservative, one who wants no change

mossel *n* : morsel

mother-baby *n* : boy or man unhappy away from home

mother-bunch *n* : a short, stout girl

Mother said I was slow but she never said I was stupid *phr* : a warning to beware what you say next

mother's mark *n* : stain on face or body of a newborn child

motion *n* : an intestinal discharge

mott *n* : clump of trees

mought *v* : might

mought could *v* : might be able to

mountain boomer *n* **1:** one from the outlying districts **2:** an uncouth person **3:** a large brightly colored lizard found in the south-central U.S. and Mexico

mountain oysters *n* : testicles of pigs

mourner's bench *n* : bench near the altar where mourners may kneel

mouse *v* : to hunt out, as a cat hunts mice

mouse-bush *n* : the pussy-willow

mouth organ *n* : harmonica

Mrs. Jones *phr* : going to the privy or toilet <He going to see ~ behind that tree.>

mubble-squibble *v* : to tease someone by running one's knuckles through the victim's hair

much *v* : coax <He ~ the dog.>

much 'blige *phr* : much oblige, a common way to say thanks

muck of sweat *n* : excessive perspiration

muckle-dun *adj* : muddy-brown

muckle to it *v* : to work hard

muda grass *n* : Bermuda grass

mudge *v* : merge

mudsill *n* : derogatory term for Yankee

mud turkle *n* : mud turtle

mulbriland *n* : Mulberry Island, in eastern Virginia

muley, mully *n* : cow that has never had horns

mulligrubs *n* : pain in the intestine, an ill temper, the sulks, the blues

mully grubs *n* : despondency <In the ~.>

multiply words *v* : whine or argue with parents when told to do something

mumbledy-peg *n* : game with two-bladed knife

mumchance *n* **1:** one who hasn't a word to say for himself **2:** a fool

mumlin-peg *n* : mumble-the-peg, the game of mumbledy-peg

mummick *v* : to cut awkwardly, mess, or make a mess of

mummy *n* : a pulpy mass

mun *n* : a familiar term of address applied to members of either sex and of any age, usually at the end of a sentence and practically expletive <Mind what I'm telling you, ~.>

munts *n* : months

murd *n* : mud

murkle *n* : myrtle, name of a tree

mushroon, musheroon, mushyroom *n* : mushroom

musicioner *n* : musician

musicker *n* : musician

muss *n* : state of confusion, disorder, a squabble, a row

mussel-head *n* : one who is slow-witted

mussy *interj* : mercy

mustydines *n* : muscadine grapes

mutton-ham sail *n* : triangular sail used in a bug-eye, a type of Chesapeake Bay boat

- N -

nabel *n* : navel

nachelly *adv* : naturally

nair, nar *adj* : narrow

nairy *adv* : not any

nake *n* : neck

nanan *n* : grandmother

nanny tea *n* : a folk remedy, made by boiling sheep manure in water

nap o'sleep *n* : a little sleep

to go napper's home *phr* : to go to sleep

narce *adj* : nice

narn *n* : nairy one

narves, narvy *n* : nerves

nary *adv* : not any

natural-born *adj* : by nature, having talent

naturalized *adj* : accustomed <We got ~ to having them visit every Sunday afternoon.>

Nawlins *n* : New Orleans

nawth *n* : above the Mason-Dixon line, where Yankees live

naysay *n* : a refusal, also right or opportunity of refusal

nearabout, nearly about *adv* : almost, nearly

near-bys *n* : neighbors

near cut, nigh cut *n :* a short byway

neckhankercher *n* : a necktie

neckid *adj* : naked

necks *adv* : next

need-be *n* : a necessity

needcessity *n* : necessity

neighbor *v* : to exchange labor, as at harvest time

neighborhood road *n* : a byway

nero *n* : zero

nervous as a whore in church *phr* : very nervous

nervous salad *n* : gelatin salad

nesses, nestes *n* : nests

never heard tell *phr* : never heard

never hit a lick *phr* : has done no work at all

newby, nooby *n* : long scarf wrapped twice around the neck

New York minute *n* : a jiffy; less than 30 seconds

nibby *adj* : too curious

nick *n* : a pile of wood

Nick, Old Nick *n* : the Devil

nicker *v* : to whinny

nicket *n* : small amount of articles, like sugar and flour

nigh *adj* : stingy

nigh cut *n* : a back road, usually a narrow trail, a shortcut

nigh onto *adv* : getting close

night-rail *n* : a night gown

nines *n* : a high degree of comparison <Up to the ~.>

nipcheese *n* : a niggardly person

nippety nip *adv* or *adj* : implies an equal sharing

nirly *n* : good-humored, but rough-spoken person

niver *adv* : never

no count *adj* : worthless

nohow *adv* : any how

noise *adj* : nice

no kin *phr* : no kidding

no'm *phr* : no ma'am

non't *v* : don't know <I ~ know.>

nooby *n* : see **newby**

noodle *v* **1:** to catch fish with one's hands **2:** to catch fish using a noodlin' hook

noodlin' hook *n* : long-handled, barbed hook to catch fish, usually by reaching into holes along a river bank where the fish have hidden

Norah *n* : Noah

norate *v* : to spread a rumor, spread a report, gossip, make public by word of mouth

noration *n* : a rumor

North Carolina heartburn *n* : when the seat of one's trousers sticks to the body

North Carolina robin *n :* a slab of salted roe-herring

Northy *adj* : sloping to the North

norty *adj* : naughty

nose out of joint *phr* : be in a bad mood

no such thing *phr* : no <Did I say you could have another piece of cake? ~!>

not about to *phr* : not going to

no telling *n* : uncertainty <There ain't ~ what he's gonna do.>

nothard *adv* : northward

nothing nohow *n* : double negative used occasionally for emphasis <Nobody can't hardly see ~.>

nothing to write home about *phr* : something inconsequential

noting *n* : nothing

notionate *adj* : given to hobbies, impulses, or whims

noways *adv* : in no way, not at all

not worth his salt *phr* : close to being worthless

nubbin killer *n* : thunder

numbrell *n* : umbrella

nuss 1: *n* nurse **2:** *v* to nurse, especially a child

nuther *adj* **1:** another **2:** neither

- O -

oak-apple *n* : oak gall, a growth on an oak tree

oak winter *n* : a late spring frost

oben *n* : oven

obleege *v* : to oblige

obstropolous *adj* : obstinate, resisting

ochestry *n* : orchestra

odd-come-short *n* **1:** an indefinite time **2:** an odd moment **3:** someday soon to come, sometime, any time

oddling *n* : something peculiar or abnormal in a harmless, inoffensive way

oddments *n* : odds and ends

of a mind to *phr* : about to do something <I'm ~ to take those goods back.>

offals *n* : pieces of food fallen from the table

off-bear 1: *n* progeny, offspring **2:** *v* to carry off

off-casts *n* : castoffs

off-girl *n* : an illegimate girl

offscouring *n* : refuse, rejected matter

offscum *n* : something vile, refuse

ofn *prep* : off of

oh hush *interj* : expression of surprise

oint *v* : to annoint, smear

oiland, oyland *n* : island

okry, oker *n* : okra

old batch *n* : bachelor

Old Boy *n* : Satan —*Var* Old Red, Old Rip, Old Sam, Old Coaley, Old Ned, Old Harry, the Other One, the Dark Stranger, Harry Scratch, Old Scratch, Old Horny, Old Blackie, Old Samson, Old Jimson

old boy *n* : one's father

Old Christmas *n* : January 6th, still observed in some places

old field *n* : cleared land

oldfields colt *n* : illegitimate child

Old Hannah *n* : the sun

old heads *n* : old people

old Joe *n* : syphillis

old lady *n* : a wife

old man *n* : husband, father, usually used respectfully

Old Master *n* : God, sometimes Jesus

old Ned *n* : fat pork, home-cured bacon

Old Scratch *n* : Satan

old soldiers *n* : ends of cigars, wads or quids of chewing tobacco

old stager *n* : some person, animal, or thing that has been long in use

Old Stoney Lonesome *n* : death

old-wife *n* : alewife, a boney fish

old woman *n* : wife at any age, usually used respectfully. Sometimes pronounced "ol' lummon"

on a credit *phr* : on credit

once and occasionally *adv* : now and then

oncle *n* : uncle

onconsarned *adv* : unconcerned

onct *adv* : once

onding *n* : a pelting rain

ondress *v* : undress

one-horse *advj* : petty, inferior, on a small scale <That's just a ~ town.>

one-poster *n* : a bed built in the corner of a cabin so that only one post is needed

on his own hook *phr* : on his own initiative

onless *adv* : unless

onliest *adv* : only, only one

onset *n* : a fight

on't *v* : won't, will not

ontelling *adj* : erratic, unpredictable

onter *prep* : onto

on the fin *n* : fresh fish caught and sold on the spot

on the floor, on the carpet *phr* : a couple being married

on the halves *phr* : split the cost two ways

ontied **1:** *v* untied **2:** *n* an unruly person

oodles *n* : a lot <There's ~ of time left.>

oojit-nawsty *adj* : good, pleasing, satisfying

ooman *n* : woman

opadeldoc *n* : soap liniment

opbrade *v* : to upbraid

open-sow *n :* a sow left unspayed to breed

open weather *n* : weather in winter when water and ground are not frozen

opry *n* : opera

orance *n* : a mysterious animal

ordinary *n* : a tavern, eating house

oreweed *n* : seaweed washed ashore and used for fertilizer; sea ore

orey-eyed *adj* : bleary-eyed

ornery *adj* : ordinary, used contemptuously

ornary 1: *n* a tavern **2:** *adj* ordinary

orphant *n* : orphan

orphline *n* : orphan

orter *n* : otter

ortherized *adj* : authorized

osnbrig *n* : osnaburg, a coarse cotton cloth

ossifer *n* : officer

other ways *adv* : otherwise

other-world *n* : world of the bad, world to come

ought to could *v* : should

ourn *pron* : ours

out *v* **1:** to cheat, defraud **2:** *prep* : off

outcry *n* : an auction

outcure *n* : a remedy used to cure more people than any other medicine

outdacious *adj* : audacious, outrageous

out-doinest *adj* : most surprising

out-dugan *v* : to outwit, get the better of, to beat

outed *v* : put out, extinguish a fire

outen *adv* : out of

outface *v* **1:** to face, comfort overbearingly **2:** browbeat

outfavor *v* : to be better look-ing than someone else

out of heart *v* : discouraged

out of whack *adj* : doesn't work, broken

outside women *n* : girlfriends of a married man

ovair *n* : over there

ovalls *n* : overalls

oven *n* : a covered iron vessel for cooking

oven bread *n* : a kind of corn bread

over, overed *v* : to recover from <I have ~ my sick-ness.>

overbraeden *v* : to overshad-ow, spread over

overhalls *n* : overalls

overlay *v* : to kill by crushing or suffocation

over yonder *n* : over there

owin' *v* : lacking, used when telling time <It's ~ 15 min-utes of five.>

own the corn *v* : to admit an error

ozark *v* : to cheat, defraud

- P -

pad *n* **1:** path <to be on the pad> **2:** to be on the go

paddy whack *n* : an Irishman

pains *n* : pins

pair *n* : a considerable num-ber, a set of things

pair of beads *n* : a string of beads

pahdon *n* : pardon

painter, panter *n* : panther

palamity *n* : many words about nothing

pallet *n* : a quilt or blanket spread on a floor as a bed

palmeeter *n* : palmetto

paper shaver *n* : person who discounts paper

pappers *n* : peppers

pappy *v* : to beget

paps *adv* : perhaps

parched *v* : roasted

parrot-toed *adj* : pigeon-toed

parsley-bed *n* : where chil-dren come from; children are often told babies are dug out of the parsley-bed

parson *n* : person

parster *n* : pasture

parze *v* : parse, as in describing the parts of speech in a sentence

pasley *n* : parsley

pasnip *n* : parsnip

pas'on *n* : parson

passel *n* **1:** parcel **2:** a lot

pass some time *v* : visit

paster *n* : pasture

pat *v* : part

patch *n* : a field

not a patchin' *phr* : by no means equal or comparable

patent *n* : land document

patron *n* : pattern

patteroll *n* : patrol

patteroller *n* : patroller —*Var* paddyroller

pattiwhack *n* : cartilage in beef

paunch *v* : punch

paw-pawer *n* : an outlaw, a fugitive

pay no mind *v* : disregard

pay-roll *n* : parole

peach leather *n* : peaches crushed, spread out, and dried

peachtree tea *n* : punishment by being whipped with a peach tree switch

peaked *adv* : sickly

pear, pears *v* : appears

pearten up *v* : to seem more lively, to go more briskly

peckerwood *n* **1:** woodpecker **2:** a derogatory term for Southern whites

peckish *adj* : somewhat hungry, inclined to eat

peel *v* : to slap or spank, as a child

peeler *n* **1:** a speech or letter criticizing a person **2:** a molting crab

peep-bo *n* : a child's game, a hiding game

peepies *n* : chickens, especially chicks

peezaltree *adj* : inferior, uncultured, unsatisfactory

peg-rock *v* : to tilt backwards in chair not on rockers

pelf *n* : money, riches

pelter *n* : a storm with hail

penders, pinders *n* : peanuts

pennyciders *n* : appendicitis

penny-piece *n* : small thing or person

pennywinkle, pinnywinkle *n* : periwinkle, a small snail

pensy *adj* : reflective, thoughtful

percoon *n* : pecan

periauger *n* : canoe made from a single log with built-up sides

perry *n* : fermented liquor made from pear juice

personate *v* : to call by name, to designate specifically

perspective glass *n* : magnifying glass, spy-glass

pert, peart *adj* : feeling well

pert near *adv* : nearly

pestle-tail *n* : an indifferent person

pet *n* : a fit, ill-humor

peter-grievous *n* : a dismal person

pethy *adj* : pithy

petrifaction *n* : a marble statue

pewter-eyed *adv* : gray-eyed, generally used disparagingly

phthisic *n* : croup

physic **1:** *v* to heal **2:** *n* a medicine

piazza *n* : a porch

pick a crow *v* : find fault with

pick-fiddle *n* : a guitar

pick-fiddle

picking geese *n* : snowfall

piddle *v* : to waste time, to do nothing in particular

piddle diddle *v* : procrastinate

pieded, piedy *adj* : spotted

pie-print *n* : likeness

pig-trail *n* : side road

pilfer round *v* : to examine or disturb property belonging to someone else

piller *n* : a pillow

pillowbear *n* : a pillow case, pillow cover

pilot-bread *n* : a dry, hard bread used at sea

pin-basket *n* : youngest child in a family

pinchback **1:** *n* alloy used in cheap jewelry **2:** *adj* sham, spurious, bogus

pinders *n* : peanuts

pindling *adj* : ailing, weak, puny, slender, usually applied to children

pine-blank *adv* : point blank

pineries *n* : pine forests

pine straw *n* : pine needles

pinetop *n* : cheap, unadulterated whiskey, said to be made of pine needles

pinginnet *n* : a facial pimple

pin-hooker *n* : an itinerant trader

pink-eye gravy *n* : gravy made from ham or other pork, to which water or milk has been added; same as red-eye gravy, black-eye gravy

pint *n* : point

pin-toed *adj* : pigeon-toed

pintoot *n* : nickname given to a boy

piny, piny rose *n* : peony

pip *v* : to crack the eggs in hatching

pipjinny *n* : a pimple, a small boil

pisoliver *n* : a revolver

pissabed *n* : dandelion. Reportedly, children who pull one will wet their beds

piss-ant *n* : ant

pissant *n* : a contemptible person

piss-clam *n* : squirting clam

pitch a crop *v* : plant a crop

pitch a fit *v* : throw a tantrum

pitcher *n* : picture

pitcher show *n* : a movie

pitch gab *v* : to make flirtatious or suggestive remarks

pitch it up *v* : to put more pep into it, sometimes referring to dancing

pizen *n* : poison

planter's pace *n* : gallop

plashy *adj* : watery, full of puddles

play-day *n* : a day exempt from work

played out *v* : exhausted

playit *n* : plate

playlike *v* : pretend

playment *n* : a toy, a play thing, a play-pretty

play-party *n* : a dance at which there is no instrumental music

play-pretty *n* : a toy, perhaps homemade

play smash *v* : to make a great blunder, do a thing wholly wrong

play whaley *v* : to blunder, fail, to make a ludicrous error

pleasure *v* : to please, indulge in pleasure

plegged *adj* : troublesome, annoying

plenty *adv* : quite

plodge *v* : to walk in water or mud, to plunge

pluck *n* : a dish made of liver, innards, sweetbreads, heart, lungs, usually from sheep or beef

plug *n* : chewing tobacco

pluggy *adj* : frail and puny

plumb *adv* : degree of something, usually extreme <He's ~ sick.>

plumper *n* : an unqualified lie, a downright falsehood

plumps *n* : game of marbles, the marble shot cannot bounce

plunder *n* **1:** household effects **2:** personal effects **3:** baggage, luggage

poach *n* : porch

pocasin, pocoson, poquoson *n* : swamp

pocket-pistol *n* : small liquor flask

pod *n* : belly, paunch

poddin, pod'n *n* : pardon

poe, po *adj* : poor

poet *v* : pour it <She took my whiskey and ~ out.>

poke *n* : pork

poke *n* : a small bag or sack

poke along *v* : move slowly

poke easy *n :* a lazy, slow person

hold the wrong end of the poker *v* : be on the losing side; make a bad bargain

poke salad *n* : cooked pokeweed

poke-sallet *n* : young, tender leaves of pokeweed used as a salad

pokeweed *n* : a plant used as a salad

pokeweed religion *n* : sort of religious fervor that springs up rapidly, seems impressive, but has no permanent value —*Var* lightning bug revivals, cocklebur saints, toadstool churches, lunch-break parsons

pole around *v* : go from place to place; usually used to refer to small boys

pole-buster *n* : a very large fish

police *v* : please

polly-fox *v* **1:** to move quietly or stealthily, to pussyfoot **2:** to dilly-dally, waste time

pomarie *n* : orchard, fruit garden

pomper *v* : pamper

pone *n* : loaf or cake of bread made of corn meal

pon hosh *n* : grease from hog-killing mixed with corn-meal, fried and sliced

pony bread *n* : pones of corn bread

poon-tang *n* : copulation, usually said of an act between people of different races

poor, po *adj* : skinny, slender

poor-do *n* : grease, shortening —*Var* scrapple

poor do, poor soles *n* : a dumpling

poor-hog *v* : live in poverty

Poor John, Po' John *n* : a small cod or hake, dressed and salted

poor white trash, po' white trash *n* : low-class whites

poot the rug *v* : to die

pop-call *n* : a very short visit

pope's nose *n* : fleshy part of tail of a bird

pop lash *v* : whip

pop-rind *n* : a meat-rind baked crisp

poquoson *n* : wet, swampy piece of ground

porely *adv* : poorly, sickly

port-mantel *n* : small leather suitcase for carrying clothes behind a saddle or horse-back, from the French word <port manteau.>

poses *n* : posts

possum-grapes *n* : a variety of small grapes

postes *n* : posts

post-hold *n* : a forked limb driven into the ground to hold fence posts when they are sharpened with an ax

posy pot *n* : a flower-pot, often makeshift

potato stomper *n* : potato smasher

potlicker *n* : a mongrel dog

pot liquor *n* : liquid left after cooking vegetables

pottanger *n* : porringer, a small bowl usually used for cereal

pound *v* : to feed, provide footstuffs for a new preacher, to hold a party for the new preacher to bring him presents

pour-down *n* : a cloudburst, a downpour

pour-off *n* : a waterfall

poverty-poor *adj* : destitute, near starvation

po-wee, powee *n* : a yell used to call hogs

powerful *adv* : considerable, immense <~ glad to see you.>

praar *n* : prayer

prank *v* : to experiment, manipulate

preacher's seat *n* **1:** a peculiar, semirecumbent position **2:** position assumed when leaping in water, with head and feet up and buttocks down

precious *adj* : cute

precious little *adv* : very little

presny *adv* : after a while, presently

prespiration *n* : perspiration

press peach *n* : peach wood

pretties *n* : pretty toys or things

pretty *n* : any little thing of value, a toy

prezactly *adv* : combined precisely and exactly

prink *v* : to dress ostentatiously or fantastically; to get dressed up

pritty *adj* : pretty

procession *v* : mark off boundaries of land

prog *v* : forage for pickings, scraps or gleanings

prog *n* : food gotten by begging; a food beggar

progue *n* : probe

projeck *n* : plan, scheme, design

projeck *v* : to meddle with

projecking *adj* : inventive, experimenting

prop pole *n* : a clothesline pole

protolapsis *n* : a mythical ailment

proud *adv* : glad, pleased

proud-flesh *n* : unhealthy flesh in a wound or sore

pucker *n* : a fuss, state of agitation, confusion

puccoon *n* : red dye used by Indians

puddin' *v* : putting

puddle jumper *n* : country dweller

puke *n* : a native of Missouri

pull fodder *n* : pulled corn leaves, tied in bundles and hung on stalks to dry

pullikins *n* : forceps

pully bone *n* : wishbone of a fowl

pum-granny, plum-granny *n* : small, yellow-striped, fragrant gourd-like fruit, pomegranate

pummies *n* : pomace, residue of sugar cane stalks pressed in a mill

pummy *n* : ground apples in cider making

pumpkin roller *n* : country dweller

pump-knot *n* : a lump, swelling

pump ship *v* : to urinate

punch-bowl *n* : a chamber pot

puncheon *n* : short upright piece of timber, usually driven in mud or water

pungy *n* : small schooner with low log gunnel

pure *adj* : good, veritable, downright

pure dee *adj* : genuine

pure quill *n* : the genuine product, unadulterated, undiluted

push comes to shove *n* : a difficult choice

push the collar *v* : to work very hard

puss *n* : purse

pussie *n* : puzzle

pussy *adj* **1:** fat, corpulent; pursy, fattish, bay-windowed **2:** countrified, awkward

putch *v* : perch

put fire to *v* : burn

put on airs *v* : flaunting one's wealth or position

put on the dog *v* : dressing up

put the big pot in the little one *phr* : to provide extraordinary hospitality, to feed a guest unusually well

put the rug *v* : to die

putting down *v* : raining hard

putty *adj* : pretty

put up *v* : canning a lot of food

- Q -

quaggy *adj* : boggy, spongy <His yard is always ~ after a rain.>

quality folks *n* : people of high social status

qualmish *adj* : affected with nausea

quare *adj :* queer, odd

querl, quirl *n* : a twist, curl

quern *n* : a mortar, a hand mill

quietus *n* **1:** calm period in early morning or afternoon **2:** a threat to children <If you don't stop, I'm going slap a ~ on you.>

quile *n* : coil

quile up *v* : become quiet

quill *v* : to blow a tune on a simple musical instrument of reeds <He can sure ~ those tunes.>

quill-wheel *v* : to move about, to cover or patrol a large area

quire *v* : cure

- R -

rabbit 'backer *n* : dried rabbit dung sometimes mixed with tobacco to make a milder smoke

rabbit gum *n* : rabbit trap

rabbit-twister *n* : a rustic, a backwoodsman

race *n* **1:** small quantity, **2:** root <That recipe calls for the ~ of ginger.>

rack *v* : to move rapidly, to make haste

Rackensack, Rackin' Sack *n* : derisive name for Arkansan

racket store *n* : a variety store

raffle *n* : rifle

raft tide *n* : tide sufficient to float rafts

raggeds *n* : rough, hilly country

rags-and-jags *n* : tatters, fragments

raid *n* : red

rain crow *n* : a bird whose cry is supposed to indicate rain

rainseed *n* : brownish, mottled clouds

raise it *v* : to begin singing a song

raise sand *v* : to start a commotion

rallack *v* : rollick

ramack *v* : to search, to ransack

ram-cat *n* : male cat

ramie *n* : a young calf

ramp *n* : wild garlic or onion

ramp, rampe *v* : to rush wildly about in a search for women

rampooch *v* : to engage in a kind of horseplay in which a boy is seized by his arms and legs and his buttocks swung violently against a tree

ramptious *adj* : wild, active, dangerous, like a mad bull

ramus *n* : ignoramus

rambunctious *adj* : unmanageable, disagreeable

randevoo *n* : rendezvous

rank *adj* : decided, strong in principle <He is a ~ Democrat.>

rap-full *adj* : full of wind, applied to sails

rapper *n* : an extravagant oath or lie

rappere *n* : a strong kind of snuff

rareripe *adj* : early ripe, hardly ripe

rassle *v* : to wrestle

rat *n* : freshman in a Southern college

rat cheer *phr* : right here

rathers *n* : choice, preference

rations *n* : food

rat smart *adj* : right smart

raven *adj* : ardent <He's so ~ about her he can't sleep nights.>

rawhead *n* : a specter or imaginary goblin used to frighten children to behave

razorback *n* : a thin, rangy, half-wild hog found in Arkansas and other neighboring Southern states

read after *v* : read about

read one's plate *phr* : say grace at the table <Will you read your plate before we eat?>

read out *v* : rebuke strongly

really *adv* : real

Rebel yell *n* : yell given by Southern troops in a charge. Renditions are attempted now during football games involving Southern schools

receipt *n* : recipe

recken *v* : believe

reckon so *v* : guess so

red betty *n* : a small whip kept as a warning, occasionally used

redding comb, reddening comb *n* : an ordinary heavy comb —*Var* booger comb

reddy-bird *n* : redbird

redeye *n* : strong, fiery whiskey, so-called because of effects on the drinker

red-eye *n* : someone obviously guilty, caught red-handed

redeye gravy *n* : gravy made from juice of cooked country ham

red lane *n* : the throat

redneck *n* : class of people just below poor whites; a derogatory term

red the guts *v* : clean the intestines at hog-killing time

reduct *v* : to subtract

red up *v* : to clean, to put in order, as a room or table

redworm *n* : a fishing worm

regiment *n* : a large number or quantity

remblings *n* : remnants

rensh *v* : to rinse

resh *v* : rush

residenter *n* : an oldtimer living at a permanent location

resk *v* : risk

restin' powder *n* : a powder used to ease pain, usually a headache

retch *v* : reach

revenooers, revenuers *n* : government agents looking for illegal stills

reverend *n* : strong, undiluted whiskey —*Var* reverent

rheumety *n* : rheumatism

ribet *n* : rivet

ribey *adj* : poor, skinny

ribbit *n* : rivet

rib-roast *v* : to beat soundly, cudgel, thrash

rib-roaster *n* : a heavy blow to the ribs

rib-roasting *n* : a beating

rick *n* : a pile of fire wood eight feet long, four feet high, and wide as the length of the logs

rick up *v* : to pile wood in an orderly manner

ricollect *v* : recollect

ride bug-hunting *v* : to ridicule, also to administer a sound thrashing

riddle *n* : a sieve, for grain, sand

riddlings *n* : coarser part of anything left in a sieve or riddle

ride shank's mare *phr* : walk —*Var* ride shank's colt

ridgeling *n* : a horse or mule with one testicle removed

ridge-runner *n* : a derisive term for a mountaineer

rifle *n* : raffle

rifle-run *n* : rifle

rig *n* : a moonshine still

rig *n* : a trick

right many, right much *adv* : very much

right smart 1: *adj* long, large, extensive **2:** *n* a considerable amount <I raised a power of corn, sold a heap, and had a ~ left.>

rigmaree *n* : a trifle, derives from a small coin minted by England in the 16th century to honor Queen Mary (Regina Maria)

rim-neck *v* : to destroy, to dismantle, to ruin

rinch *v* : rinse

rino *n* : money

rip *n* : a vicious, reckless, and worthless person

rip and stare *v* : to range and scold about

ripshin *n* : a briar, or a bush having briars

ription *n* : a contraption

the rise of *phr* : slightly more than

risin' *n* : a boil, an abscess

risk *adj* : outrageous, preposterous

riverjack *n* : rock from a river bed

roach *v* : to comb the hair so that it stays fixed; to comb the hair back from front, smooth and straight

roach *n* : cowlick of hair

roasting ear *n* : ripe, mature corn; also applied to other plants

roasting ear peas *n* : a legume

rock *v* : to throw stones

rock-house *n* : a shallow cave or shelter under an overhanging bluff

rode hard and put up wet *phr* : exhausted after a long day

roger *v* : to copulate

rogerry *n* : the penis

roguish *adj :* term applied to cattle that break through fences

rollix *v* : to frolic, to carouse, philander

roly-mole *n* : game of marbles

romble *v* : ramble

romp *n* : a rude girl who indulges in boisterous play

root hog or die *phr* : look out for yourself

rosnears *n* : roasting ears of corn

rossel *v* : to wrestle

rosum *n* : rosin

rotgut *n* : bad or unadulterated whiskey; strong, bad liquor

rough *n* **1:** roof **2:** a grove, a thicket

rough as a cob *phr* : uncultured and uneducated

roughness *n* : roughage or fodder

rouser *n* **1:** a healthy, hefty baby **2:** a fine, large fish

rubbage *n* : rubbish

ruction *n* : a quarrel, fight, uproar

ruddy *adj* : ready

rue back *v* : to back down from a bargain; to cancel a bargain, to trade back

ruff *n* : rough

ruffle *v* : to prune

rullion *n* : a coarse, tough, unkempt person, usually a woman of low morals

rullock *n* **1:** oarlock on a boat **2:** a rag, tattered garment

rum *n* : room

run *n* : a stream

runabout *n* : a gadabout, vagabond

run a rig *v* : to play a joke or trick on someone

run like a scalded dog *v* : run fast

runnet *n* : the stomach, sometimes the gall bladder

runt *v* : ruined

rush-bottom *n* : seat made of rushes

rusky *adj* : satisfactory

rustes *n* : rust

rusty *adj* : rancid <That ~ bacon has been sittin' around for weeks.>

ruts *n* : roots

- S -

sacer *n* : saucer

Sadday *n* : Saturday

saddle-backed *adj* : sway-backed

safe *n* : receptacle for storing meat and provisions

sager *n* : a would-be wise man

Sah, Suh *n* : Sir

sallet *n* : greens, salad of greens

salvatory *n* : a place where things are preserved

same like *adv* : just like, just as

sanctum suly *n* : good whiskey

sand-bugger *n* : a kind of food made of potatoes and onions

sand hiller *n* : native of eastern South Carolina and Georgia

sandy *n* : a trick, a bluff

sane *n* : a saying

sang *n* : ginseng

sangaree *n* : red wine diluted with water, sweetened and flavored with nutmeg

sanging *v* : gathering ginseng

sang root *n* : ginseng

sanko *v* : to walk silently, to pussyfoot around with no apparent purpose

sanks *v* : sleep

sanky poke *n* : a traveling bag

sarch *v* : to search

sarment *n* : a sermon

sartin *adj* : certain

sarvant *n* : servant

sarve *v* : to serve

services *n* : fruit of the service berry tree

sarvis *n* : service

sash-light *n* : a pane of glass in a window

sashay *v* : to parade, strut about

saspan *n* : saucepan

sass *n* **1:** backtalk **2:** sauce **3:** garden vegetables

sassafac, sassafrack *n* : sassafras

sassage, sassinger *n* : sausage

sasser *n* : saucer

Satan's mark *n* : five small pits in the skin on the inside of the foreleg of a hog

saucered and blowed *v* : hot coffee cool enough to drink

save *v* : to house a crop

save-all *n* : candlestick pan

sawder *n* : flattery, blarney

saw off a whopper *v* : to tell a tall tale, to spin a boastful story

saw on (one's) gourds *v* : to snore

say *v* : speak lessons

scadoodles *n* : a very large number, a very large amount; combination of scads and oodles

scaffling *n* : scaffolding

scald-head *n* : eczema

scaley *adv* and *adj* : inferior, low grade, contemptible

scamp *v* : to graze, touch lightly in passing

scantling *n* : wood cut to special sizes for carpenter's use

scape-gallows *v* : to idle about, to loaf

scaper *n* : a rascal

scarce as hen's teeth *phr* : virtually non-existent

scarce-hipped *adv* : slender

scarce of *adv* : lacking, short of

scare up *v* : to locate <See if you can ~ some drinks.>

scarify *v* : to frighten, scare

scary-crow *n* : scarecrow

scase *n* : scarce

scaths *n* : having loss, damages

scatteration *n* : a dispersal, a scattering

schnitts and kanaps *n* : fried apples wrapped in dough and dropped in boiling water

school butter *n* : used as a term of reproach to school children

schum *v* : schemed

science *adj* : skillful, proficient, expert

scoffle *v* : to ridicule, scoff

scoop-town *adv* : an emphatic affirmative, comparable to "sure."

scope *n* : a tract or piece of land <He owned a mighty ~ of land.>

score *n* : large wooden chip used for fire wood

scoripin *n* : scorpion

scot *n* : one's share of an expense

scotch 1: *v* to prop or block a wheel **2:** *n* a prop or block under a wheel

scotch for *v* : to help out

scramblance *n* : nuts and fruit thrown to children, to be scrambled for

Old Scratch *n* : the Devil

scratchback *n* : corn bread in a simple form

scraunch *v* : grind with one's teeth

screak *v* : to creak

scriber *n* : a writer, a penman

scriggle *v* : to wriggle

scrimption *n* : a small portion, a pittance

scringe *v* : to shrink from fear or dislike, to cringe

scritch-owl *n* : screech owl

scroach *v* : draw up in a small space

scrooch, scrouge, scroonch, scrunch *v* : to crouch, squeeze oneself into a close place, press

scrop *n* : scrap

scrumptious *adv* : best

scrunch *v* : to crunch, crush with the teeth

scrutch *v* : to crouch

scuttle *n* : a stairway

search 1: *n* a sieve, a sieve made of horse hair **2:** *v* to sift through a sieve

sea-wrack *n* : coarse seaweeds cast on shore

section hand *n* : worker on a railroad section maintenance crew

sedlins *n* : fine clay

seetrus *n* : citrus fruit

segashiate *v* : to move about, to progress, usually jocular or facetious

sell-out *v* : to leave quickly

sep, seps *adv* : except

serenade *n* : a noisy celebration after a wedding

sermont, sermint *n* : a sermon

set-along *n* : small child able to sit alone on the floor

set a spell *v* : to visit

set-fast *n* : a hard swelling

set his cap *v* : to court

set one's budget down *v* : to come to a decision, to take a firm stand

set out *v* : to seek a husband, show a desire for marriage, usually said of widows seeking to remarry

set over *v* : to carry a person across a stream in a boat

settin'-up *n* : a wake for the dead

setting-down *n* : a rebuke

settins *n* : settlings, dregs, sediment

set up with *v* **1:** to court **2:** to sit at a wake

seven-sleepers *n* : a sleepy-headed person who is hard to wake

severe *adj* : fierce, <a ~ dog>

sewed-up *v* : to be drunk

shackelty *adj* : loosely held together, run down

shackly *adj* : shaky, tottering, ramshackle

shad-bellied *adj* : sloping away in front, usually used to describe a coat

shade *n* : a shed

shadetree mechanic *n* : a mechanic shy on skills and learning on the job

shady *adv* : beyond <He's on the ~ side of forty years old.>

shag *v* : to copulate

shag-leg *n* : loose woman

shagtail *n* : a snapping turtle

shake-down *n* : a makeshift bed, a pallet laid on the floor

shaking-ague *n* : a violent fever

shaller **1:** *v* to become shallow **2:** *v* *n* high pitch <She started the tune too ~.>

shallot *n* : a small onion

shalves, sharves *n* : shafts

shammick *v* : to lounge about idly

shammock *v* : to walk in a slouch, unsteady manner

shammy *n* : chamois

shank's mare *n* : on foot

shank of the evening *n* : late afternoon

shank's ponies, to ride *v* : to walk

shape notes *n* : the peculiar notation some mountain singing teachers, especially those in the Ozarks, used rather than ordinary music notes; sometimes called "buckwheat music"

share crop *n* : land rented to a tenant for shares of the tenant's crop

sharecropper *n* : tenant who farms land on shares

shares, on the shares *phr* : applied to renting land by payment of fixed share of profits

sharp-set *v* : hungry and ready for one's food

shatters *n* : pine needles on the ground

shawt *n* : short

shear *n* : share

sheckly *adj* : shaky

she-crab soup *n* : rich soup made from crabmeat

sheep dumplings *n* : sheep manure

shelly *adj* : inferior, of low grade, in poor condition

shelly beans *n* : a legume, dried beans

shell the brush, shell the woods *phr* : lot of speech-making and hand-shaking in a political race

sheltery *adv* : said of a place that affords shelter

shenamugan *n* : stunt

sherk, shirk *n* : shark, a fish

sherry-vallies *n* : thick cloth leggings used in riding, to keep off mud

shet *v* : shut

sheth *n* : sheath

shettle *n* : shuttle as used on a loom

shield *n* : sheath, scabbard

shifty *adj* : alert

shike poke, shitepoke *n* : green heron; sometimes called "fly-up-the-creek"

shimmy *n* : chemise

shindig *n* : a dance

shindy *n* : a row, disturbance, or rumpus

shirtmen *n* : Virginia militia in the Revolutionary War. Name applied by the British because the Virginians wore hunting shirts

shirt-tail boy *n* : a very young boy

shivaree *n* : charivari; a noisy, mock celebration after a wedding, a boisterous party for newlyweds

shiver *v* : to propel, throw, to fire

shivers *n* : small pieces, slivers <The cup broke into ~.>

sho, shore *adv* : sure

shoal *v* : to assemble for breeding or spawning, as fish do; applied also to humans

shoat *n* : person of little value

shocky *n* : salt

shoemake *n* : sumac, sumack

shoe-mouth deep *n* : snow, water, or mud that is deep enough to come to the top of one's shoe

shoe-tie *n* : shoe string

shon't *v* : contraction for shall not

shoo-fly *n* **1:** big bow of ribbon which some elderly women wear as a neck tie **2:** a hair style combed low on the forehead with the ends brushed back

shool *v* : to waste time doing a task

shoot **1:** *v* belittle, often used with down <I'll tell you my idea if you promise not to ~ it down.> **2:** *n* a person nearly mature

shootin'-fixin's *n* : firearms and ammunition

shoowit *v* : shoot

short-cake *n* : corn bread made by putting grease in it

short commons *n* : scant supplies or provisions

short-horn *n* : an ordinary person

shorts *n* **1:** a side of bacon **2:** the coarse, glutinous part of ground wheat

short sweeting *n* : sugar; long sweeting is molasses or honey

shotgun house *n* : a house with rooms all in a row

shot my wad *v* : finished

shotten *adj* : dislocated, as in a bone

showery *adv* : many showers

show-out *v* : show off

shreeve *n* : sheriff

shuckle *v* : to hurry, bustle about

shur *v* : to share, also, to shear

shut-mouth *n* : one who says little about his or her personal affairs

shut my mouth *interj* : what all Yankees think Southerners say as an expression of surprise or wonder

sib *adv* : akin to, having similar tastes, likes

Side-Hill Hoofer, Side-Hill Slicker, Side-Hill Walloper *n* : a mythical beast that runs around mountaintops always in the same direction so its legs on one side are longer than the others

sidelin' *adj* : leaning, inclined, not horizontal

side-line *v* : to catch fish by forcing them to jump in the boat

side meat, side pork *n* : bacon or salt pork

sidesman *n* : assistant to church warden

side-wipe *n* **1:** a sly rebuke **2:** a bastard

siege *n* : a long time

sift *v* : to travel fast, go in a hurry

signify *v* : to show off

sile *n* : soil

simlin *n* : cymblin, a small, edible gourd

simmer down on *v* : to concentrate, specialize in

simmon beer *n* : beverage made using persimmons

simon *n* : salmon

singing convention *n* : a singing contest of local groups of hymn singers

sink-taller whiskey *n* : liquor of a high alcoholic content. If a lump of tallow will float in whiskey, the whiskey is weak, but if it sinks, whiskey is strong

sippin' whiskey *n* : the best bourbon, usually only opened for good friends

siss *v* : to hiss

sister *n* : a woman —*Var* sister woman

sistren *n* : sisters of a society or guild

sithence *prep* : since

sivvy beans *n* : butter beans, lima beans

sizz *v* : to hiss, sizzle

sizzly-sozzly *n* : very light rain

skearce *adj* : scarce

skear-crow *n* : scarecrow

skeart *n* : skirt

skeer *v* : to scare

skeet *v* : skate

skeletum *n* : skeleton

skelp *v :* to scalp

skelter-eyed, skeller-eyed *adv* : crosseyed

skiff *n* : light snowfall

skift *n* : thin layer of snow

skift *n* : sled or sledge used in hauling stone

skig *n* : skeg, the part of a boat's keel on which the rudder is mounted

skileton *n* : skeleton

skillet blonde *n* : a very black woman

skillpot *n* : red-bellied terrapin

skinny-grievous *adj* : thin, scrawny

skint *adj* : skinned

skipper *n* : certain larvae in spoiled bacon and cheese

skippery *adv* : abounding in skippers

skitters *n* : diarrhea

skunt *v* : skinned

skyhootin' *adv* : excessive or out of sight <Prices have gone ~ way up next to what a farmer gets for his crops.>

sky-gogglin' *adv* : crooked, irregular, lopsided, askew, aslant, awry —*Var* skeewaddlin', sky-waddlin', sky-wampus

sky-windin' *adv* : a great distance

sky-ways *adj* : crooked, askew

slabber *n* : slobber

slab-sided *adj* : tall and lank

slantendicular *adj* : not quite vertical, slanting

slap-up *adj* : excellent, first-rate, fine

slashes *n* : shallow pools of water left after a rain

slashways *adv* : diagonally

slat-bonnet *n* : a sunbonnet whose brim has a cloth stitched in rows to form pockets in which strips of cardboard can be inserted

slathers *n* : a very large amount

slattery *adj* : dirty, dilapidated, in poor condition

slaunch *n* : an angle, usually sawed by guess <I guess that's about the right ~.>

slaunchways *adj* : diagonal, slanting, not level, not straight

slick *n* **1:** a minnow **2:** an impassable thicket of laurel or rhododendron —*Var* hell or yaller patch

slick as a ribbon *adv* : completely <He got out of that deal ~.>

slicker *v* : to beat, flog severely

slickside *n* : a large, sloping rock

slight *n* : a knack or skill

slip up *v* : to miscarry, a miscarriage

slipper spoon, slipper slide *n* : a shoe horn

slue *n* : many

slued *adj* : slightly drunk

slump *n* : a large, fleshy, untidy person

slut *n* : a primitive lamp made by tying a rag wick to a pebble and putting it in a vessel of grease

smack *adv* : at once <Go ~ and do it now!>

smack-dab *adv* : squarely, exactly

smack out of *adv* : completely out of something <I'm ~ beer.>

smearcase *n* : cheese made of curd and sour milk; cottage cheese

smellers *n* : a cat's whiskers

smell the patching *v* : to be involved in spirited conflict or struggle; derived from being close enough to muzzle-loaded gunfire to smell the patching burning

smidgen *n* : a small amount, a bit

smur *n* : a heavy fog

snake-doctor *n* : a dragonfly

snake-doctor

snake-dried *n* : skin dried and hardened from sitting near the fire

snap beans *n* : string beans

snapper *n* : snapping turtle

snatch *n* : female genitals

snawfus *n* : a legendary creature thought to be like an albino deer with great white wings and flowering boughs for antlers

sneck *n* : a snake

snewed *v* : snowed

snibbling *adv* : dark, cloudy, raining

snickup *n* : to sneeze, as a cat

snide *v* : to bamboozle

snipperty *adj* : insignificant, ridiculously small

sniptious *adj* : smart and finicky

snit *n* : a weeping fit, a tantrum

snits *n* : apples, quartered to let dry

snoah, snow *v* : to snore

snobscat *n* : a cobbler of shoes

snubbing *v* : sobbing

snud, snudding *n* : a hurry, a rush

snuffles *n* : sniffles

snuff-mop *n* : chewed twig used in dipping snuff, usually peach or black-gum —*Var* swab, snuff stick

soaky *n* : a biscuit soaked in sweetened coffee

sobby *adj* : soggy, heavy, underdone, also wet, mouldy

sockdologer *n* **1:** a conclusive argument **2:** something large, a whopper; something surprising in size or quality

sodle *v* : to make no progress

sog *adj* : too wet <That wood's ~ and won't burn.>

soft-mouth, sweet talk *v* : to pacify

solid fellow *n* : suitor with serious matrimonial intentions

som'ers *adv* : somewhere

some kind of *adv :* really, truly <He's ~ smart.>

something on a stick *n* : something unusually fine or valuable, usually said facetiously <She thinks she's ~.>

sonker *n* : fruit cobbler

soo *n* : suet, fat of beef, or mutton

soojet *n* : sack, pouch

sooky *n* : a cow

sooner *n* : child born less than nine months after its parents wed

sooner dog *n* : mongrel

soot *n* : suit of clothes

soozy *adj* : countryfied or uncouth and at the same ludicrously conceited

sop *n* : gravy, usually from pork

sorghum *n* : a syrup

sorghum lapper *n* : a country dweller

sorry *adj* : inferior, squalid

sot *v* : set, sit

sot-work *n* : knitting, mending, needlework that can be done sitting down

soul-case *n* : the body

soup-bone *n* : arm

sour gnat *n* : any sort of insect that gets in one's eyes

southron *n* : southern

sow belly *n* : pork from the belly or low side of a pig; bacon, salt pork

sow-cat *n* : she cat

sowcoon *n* **1:** jocular name for a cyclone **2:** a female raccoon

spang *n* : gravy

spang *v* : to throw with violence

spar, sparrer, sparry *n* : sparrow

sparrables *n* : sparrowbills, small iron nails for shoes

sparrer-grass *n* : asparagus

spat *n* : spot

spell *n* : strange behavior

spew *v* : to strew, scatter

spicket *n* : faucet

spider *n* : a skillet or frying pan with three legs to keep it off the coals

spike *n* : an arrow

spile *v* : spoil

spinner *n* : spider

spit cotton **1:** *v* to be angry **2:** *n* an indication a person has drunk too much whiskey **3:** *v* to be very thirsty

spit fire new *phr* : absolutely new

splat *v* : pat, slap, spat

split the quill *v* : to separate, quarrel, fall out

split the blanket *phr* : separation of a marriage, a divorce

splosion *n* : an explosion

splot *n* : splotch, spot

spoat, spote *n* : sport

spondolics *n* : money

spoon bread *n* : a dish of cornmeal, milk, eggs, shortening

spoony *adv* : foolishly fond of something, sentimental

sporting house *n* : brothel

sprang *v* : spring

spread-nadder *n* : spreading adder, a milk snake

sprig *n* : a brad, sharp nail having no head

spring fresh *n* : a heavy rain

spring-keeper *n :* a water newt living in a spring and thought to keep the water flowing and fresh

sprout straddler *n* : a country dweller

sprung *v* : tipsy, drunk

spudding *v* : to idle, loiter, usually used with <around.>

spunk *n* : dry, partially decayed wood

spunk-water *n* : rainwater in cavities of trees or stumps

srimps *n* : shrimp

squander *v* : to scatter, disperse

square *n* : the title of squire

squash *v* : to crush

squaw-wood *n* : small or badly cut firewood

squee-jawed *adj* : distorted, misshapen, lopsided

squench *v* : to extinguish, obliterate, subdue

squib *n* : a young squirrel

squinch *v* **1:** to squint **2:** to quench

squinch owl *n* : screech owl

squirmy *n* : lively young girl

squirrel-dumplings *n* : facetious name for noodles

squirrel-turner *n* : an expert with the small rifle used in squirrel shooting

squirts, squtters *n* : diarrhea

stand table *n* : small decorative table

starn *adj* : stern

stars *n* : stairs

Stars and Bars *n* : official Confederate flag; not the battle flag

stars and garters *interj* : an exclamation, usually of surprise

start *adv* : entirely, completely <He was ~ naked.>

starve out *v* : to die, become extinct

stawk *n* : stork

stay-bit *n* : a snack, bite between meals

stay more *v* : to remain longer

steeple *n* : staple, basic food ingredient, usually flour, salt, or sugar

stent *n* : allotted portion

step off the carpet *v* : get married

stewer *n* : a stewpan

stickery *advj* : prickley, covered with sharp points or stickers

sticks to your ribs *phr* : used to describe hearty food

sticky, stickies *n* : cold biscuit split in two, buttered with molasses spread over them, then put in hot oven —*Var* taffy biscuits

stid *n* : bedstead

stiddier *adv* : instead

stink base *n* : a game of running bases

stink bird *n* : any small bird that stays close to the ground

stirrup cup *n* : last drink before leaving a place

stiver *n* : something of small value

stodge *v* : to season, to spice, to flavor

stompers *n* : large, heavy shoes

stomping ground *n* : home country <This is my ~.>

stone bruise *n* : bruise on the sole of the foot

stone-horse *n* : a stallion

stool chair *n* : any chair without rockers

stoop *n* : small porch

stop by *n* : a casual visit

store bread *n* : wheat bread

store bought *n* **1:** anything purchased from a store **2:** quality

story and a jump *n* : a house with a story and a half

stove up *n* : stiff from overwork; feeling bad <He's got a ~ back.>

stout *n* : good health

stouten *v* : to make stout

strack *v* : strike

stradways *v or n* : stride

strangth *n* : strength

strawberry friend *n* : a moocher, usually a city friend who visits his country cousins when strawberries are ripe

strean *n* : strain

strenth *n* : strength

stretch the blanket *v* : to exaggerate, tell a tall story

striffin *n* **1:** membrane which lines an eggshell **2:** tough skin which protects the body of a mussel **3:** sometimes a membrane in the human body

string beans, snaps *n* : green beans

strollop **1:** *n* rambling woman of doubtful morals **2:** *v* to wander

stroud *n* : shroud

strut *v* : to swell

studiens *n* : students

study *v* : to ponder, consider, meditate

studying *v* : considering <I ain't ~ you.>

stump-knocker *v* : traveling preacher

stump speech *n* : a political speech

stump sucker *n* : horse that chews wood

stump-tail English *n* : newspaper English

stun *n* : stone

sturp *n* : stirrup

suck-egg dog *n* : expression of contempt <He's as shifty as a ~.>

suck-egged mule *n* : expression of surprise or astonishment <I'll be a ~.>

suck hind tit *v* : get the worst of everything; to occupy a disadvantageous position <No matter what I do, I still ~.>

suddently *adv* : suddenly

sugar *n* : term of affection

sugar bread *n* : cake

sugar camp *n* : orchard of sugar maples

sugarhouse molasses *n* : a kind of table syrup

sugar-teat *n* : sugar tied in a cloth and given to infants to quiet them

sugar tree molasses *n* : maple sugar

suggin *n* : a hill dweller of inferior stock and low mentality

sukee, suk *phr* : term used in calling cows

sull *v* : to sulk

sulter *v* : to smother, suffocate, swelter, stifle

summerset *n* : somersault

sun-ball *n* : the sun

Sunday baby, Sunday child *n* : a child out of wedlock

Sunday clothes, Sunday go-to-meeting clothes *n* : one's best clothes

sun-dog *n* : a mock sun or small round halo seen on the sun's plane, a parhelion

sun pain *n* : face-ache, neuralgia in upper part of face said to come and go with the sun. Supposedly cured by hanging triangular-shaped lead piece around the neck; a severe headache

suppen *n* : something

supper *n* : the evening meal

sure is *adv* : certainly

surp *n* : syrup

suspicy *n* : suspicions

sut *n* : soot

suthard *adj* : southward

swad *n* : lump, mass, or bunch

swag **1:** *v* to lean, sag **2:** *n* a piece of low, swampy ground

swage *v* : assuage; to decrease in size, reduce a swelling

swallow-pipe *n* : the gullet

swamp dew *n* : moonshine, corn whiskey

swamp dollar *n* : large copper penny

swamp trash *n* : poor white trash

sward *n* : swarth or turf

swarved *v* : crowd, huddled

swash *v* : splash

swate *adj* : sweet

sweet-anny *n* : anise

sweet potato *n* : yams; used for starch dish, pies, soup

sweet talk *n* : flattery

sweet-wood *n :* red cedar <She keeps them fine clothes in a ~ chest.>

swiddle *v* : to stir, dip

swill *n* : drink liquor to excess

swill-tub *n* : a drunkard

swilge *v* : to wash, rinse, as <~ a churn>

swimp *n* : shrimp

swinge *v* : to singe

swingle *v :* to beat or break flax with a swingle knife

swingle knife *n* : a wooden knife used to break flax

swink *v* : shrink

switch-cane *n :* a kind of evergreen bamboo

switchel *n* : drink made from molasses and water, sometimes with vinegar and ginger

swivet *n* : a hurry, rush, as <in a ~.>

swoggle *v* : to dip, stir

swole *adj* : swollen <Her leg is all ~ up.>

swollen in a strut *adj* : severely swollen

swoom *n* : swoon

- T -

table muscle *n* : large girth, stomach

tables *n* : backgammon

tack *v* : take

tacky, tackies *adj* : unfashionable, shabby in dress, a person so characterized

tad, tat *n* : small boy

taddick *n* : small amount of coffee, sugar, other condiments

tafia *n* : inferior grade of rum

Tagger *n* : Tiger, a dog's name

take after *v* : to have illicit sexual relations <That woman will ~ anything wearin' pants.>

take down with *v* : to become ill with a specified disease

take foot in hand *v* : walk

take in, takes in *v* : to begin, as school classes <School ~ early.>

taken *v* : took

takened *v* : took, taken

take off *v* : to leave

take on *v* : to mourn loudly

take out *v* **1:** stop work, to unhitch a team from farm implement **2:** to close, let out

take rounders *v* : to walk around an obstacle

takes a toll *phr* : a burden <All that bad news ~ on you.>

take the cake *phr* : a winner <If that don't ~, I don't know what would.>

take the leavings *v* : to withdraw hurriedly

take the rag off *v :* to stop pretending

take the rag off the bush *phr* : expression of astonishment <Doesn't that ~!>

take the studs *v* : to balk, become stubborn

taking *n* : impatience, ingratiating

tal *v* : towel

talk a blue streak *v* : talk incessantly

talk short *v* : to speak angrily, contemptuously

talky *adj :* talkative

tallyho *n* : a substantial blow with the fist

tallywags *n* : a man's privates, male genitalia —*Var* tallywhacker

talpa *n* : the catalpa tree

tanglefoot *n* : moonshine whiskey

tanter *n* : tantrum

tantibogas *n* : the devil

tantivy *adj* : swift, rapid

tanty-see-bow *adv* or *adj* : satisfactory after having been otherwise <Is it ~ now?>

tar **1:** *n* : tire **2:** *v* : tear

tar-brush *n* : having black blood <There's a touch of the ~ in her.>

tar heel *n* : a North Carolinian

tarrapin *n* : terrapin

tarred *v* : tired

tarrier *n* : terrier

tarryhoot *v* : to gallivant

tase *v* : taste

tat **1:** *v* : to gossip, tattle **2:** *n* : small amount

tater grabber *n* : farmer

tater-trap *n* : the mouth

tauten *v* : to become taut, tense

taw *n* : marbles, as in playing a game of marbles <We're gonna shoot some ~ at recess.>

to come to taw *v* : to be brought to account

tea-fight *n* : a tea party

teakle *v* : tackle

tear-out *n* : a boisterous, hilarious meeting

tear the bone out *v* : to do anything thoroughly

tear up Jack *v* : to make a great commotion

teaspot, teaspout *n :* small boy's penis

techous *adj* : touchy, sensitive

teck *n* : take

tediousome *adj* : tedious

teem *v* : to pour, drain

teen *n* : ten

tee-ninchy *adj* : variant of tiny or teeny

tee-toncey *adj* : tiny

tell *prep* : 'til, until

tetchified *adv* : choleric, fretful

tetchous *adj* : tender, sensitive, easily aroused

tetchy *adj* : peevish

thang **1:** *n* : thing **2:** *v* : to thank

thanky *v* : thank you

thank you for *phr* : a polite phrase of request <I'll ~ the tomatoes.>

thar *adv* : there

thashhold *n* : threshhold

that there *pron* : that one

theah *adv* : there

them *pron* : those

there now *adv* : stay calm

these here *pron* : these

they, they's *adv* : there, there is

theyselves *pron* : them, themselves

think for *v* : suppose

this here *pron* : this

thole *v* : to endure

thort *n* : thwart

thother *adv* : the other

thought *n* : thwart, a brace or seat extending across a small craft, such as a canoe

thought the world of *v* : held in high regard <We ~ him.>

thoughty *adj* : thoughtful

tho up *v* : barf

thousands *adv* : of a large size or amount rather than a large number <Them britches is ~ big.>

thouten *prep* : without

thrash *n* : rash in a child's mouth

three sheets to the wind *adj* : very drunk

thriblets *n* : triples

thrifty *adv* : able to turn food into fat, especially by hogs

throddy *adj* : well grown, plump

through *n* : a series of doses of medicine <The doctor ordered me to take a ~ of heart pills.>

throwing the hatchet *v* : telling lies

throw off on *v* : belittle

thrums *n* : coarse yarn

thud *n* : third

thumb-buster *n* : a single-action revolver

thunder-mug *n* : a chamber pot

thusty *adj* : thirsty

tickled *v* : to be amused

tickler *n* : half pint bottle of liquor; a flat pocket flask with just enough liquor to "tickle" a thirst

ticky *adv* : describes persons in a rough or unpolished condition

tiddy-bit *n* : small portion of anything

tide *n* : a freshet or flood, especially of mountain streams <A spring ~ in these mountains will stop travel.>

tidies *n* : covering for sofa arms and back to keep them from being soiled

tidolodeum *n* : anything infinitesimal in size

tie a knot in his tail *phr* : give someone a little pain figuratively to get his attention

tie-hacker *n* : a man who hacks railroad ties with a broad-ax

tie-tongued *adv* : tongue-tied

Tige *n* : name for a dog, variation of Tiger

tight as Dick's hatband *phr* : said of someone who is miserly

tilt *n* : awning on a boat

tilting *n* : a tournament, an athletic contest

timber doodle *n* : the woodcock

timber-toes *n* : toes that are turned inward

time of books *phr* : study period in school

timersome *adj* : timid, easily frightened

by times *adv* : early, soon

tissick *n* : a cold, infection of throat and lungs

tiltivate *v* : to dress neatly

toad *prep* : toward

toad-frog *n* : a toad

toadstool churches *n* : churches formed after a summertime revival

toad strangler *n* : a heavy rain

toastes *n* : toasted bread

tod *n* : a drink

toddick *n* **1:** a portion of grain a miller took as his fee **2:** a gourd used to dip out a grain miller's toll

toe-each *n* : toe-itch

toe-party *n* : a dance

tohind, t'hind *adv* or *prep* : behind <Don't look ~ you.>

toide *n* : tide

tolable, tollible *adv* : fairly well

tolt *v* : told

tomcatting around *v* : young male looking for women

tomfuller *n* : hominy

tomor *n* : tomorrow

tomwalkers *n* : stilts

ton *v* : turn

tone *v* : torn

tonger *n* : oyster tonger, an oysterman who uses tongs to pull up his catch

tonguey *adj* : loquacious, garrulous

to one's notion *phr* : to suit or please one

toodles *n* : male child's genitals

took to her bed *v* : become bedridden with illness

took up with *v* : live together, cohabit

too poor to paint and too proud to whitewash *phr* : said of impoverished Southern gentry

toothful *n* : small drink of liquor

tooth jumper *n* : mountain dentist of the old school, who extracted teeth by means of a mallet and a slender steel punch

top hog *n* : a boar

top-of-the-pot *n* : people of the highest social or economic class, the best

top-water *n* **1:** little minnow that swims on the surface **2:** small-timer, second rate

torectly *adv* : directly, immediately, soon

torn-down *adj :* mischievous

torn-downdest *adj* **1:** wildest, most destructive, roughest **2:** toughest, most worthless **3:** violent place or thing

totch *v* : touched

tote *v* : to carry

tote fair *v* : to play fair; to act or deal fairly

tote right *phr* : to be fair, to conform to local ethics <I aim to ~ with everybody.>

tote sack *n* : a burlap bag

tother *pron* : that other, the other

tottle *v* : to totter

touch hands *v* : to unite, to cooperate, to stick together

touchous *adv* : easily angered, ill-tempered

tourer *n* : tourist

tourister *n* : tourist

tow sack *n* : burlap bag

toy *v* : tie

toy-dog *n* : small dog kept as a pet

trade howdies *v* : exchange greetings

trampoose *v* : to tramp, walk, or wander about

trance *v* : to tramp, travel

trapes *n* : a slattern, a promiscuous woman

trashy *adj* : low class

tread *v* : to copulate, as birds

treadle *v* : the bands of albumen in an egg

tree-dog *n* : dog used in hunting racoons, possums; as distinguished from a fox hound or bird dog

tree-top *v* **1:** to land a fish with unnecessary force, throwing it into the treetops **2:** to attack a project with unusual vigor or enthusiasm

trifling *adj* : shiftless, of little account

trigger up *v* : to primp, dress up

trim *v* : to castrate

trinkle, a-trinklin' *v* : to move around in an annoying manner <A gang of youn-guns was ~ around under-foot.>

tritchet *n* : female genitals

T-road *n* : a three-branch road that forms a T

troft *n* : trough

trolling *v* : walking around, rambling

trollop *n* **1:** a tramp or per-son given to idleness **2:** one who travels a great deal

tromp *v* : tramp

trots *n* : diarrhea

trotter, trotters *n* : foot, leg <He upped his ~ and knocked him flat.>

truckle *v* : to hurry, move rapidly under orders

to be true *v* : to be sure

tuck *v* : took

tuckered out *v* : exhausted

tuckey *n* : turkey

tuckin' comb *n* : comb old women wear at the back of their heads

tudder *pron* : the other

tudy-rose *n* : design used in old-time quilts and fancy needlework

tumble-turd *n* : a dung beetle

tunk *v* : to thump, rap

tup *v* : to copulate, as a ram

turkemtime *n* : turpentine

turkey-eggs *n* : freckles

turkey-tails *v* : to branch out in the shape of a fan <The creek ~ out into numerous little forks.>

turkle *n* : turtle

turn *n* : disposition, tempera-ment, kind of mind <She developed such a ~ when her child died nobody could live with her.>

turnip *n* : a pocket watch

turnip kraut *n* : shredded, pickled turnips

turn-key job *n* : a finished house

turn of the night *n* : passing midnight

turn of wood *n* : load of fire-wood

turn thanks *n* : a blessing; short for <return thanks>

turrible *adj* : terrible

tush *n* : a tusk, a long-pointed tooth

tushes *adv* : having tusks

twang *n* : something with a sharp taste, tang

twat *n* : female genitals

twell *prep* : 'til, until

twick *n* : a twitch

twigger *n* : a man or woman who cuts twigs of cedar to sell at Christmas

twinkles *n* : pine and balsam needles

twitchet *n* **1:** female genitals **2:** a fidget, a nervous fit

twitteration *n* : a twitter, a flutter

two-three *n* : a few, two or three

t-y-t *n* : a lie, derives from tittle or gossip <You said she was runnin' around and that's a ~.>

- U -

ugly *v* : to drive out <You always ~ my friends out of the house.>

Ujinctum *n* : Hell

unalike *adv* : unlike

unbeknownst *adj* or *adv* : without one's knowledge or consent; unknown

unbritch *v* : to open a breech-loading firearm

uncomeatable *adj* : unattainable

uncomfort *adj :* uncomfortable

unconvenient *adj* : inconvenient

undecent *adj* : indecent

under rail *adj* : fenced

understrapper *n* : inferior person, a servant

unfeed *v* : to defecate

unfinancial *adj :* without money

unfitten *v* : not fit

unhonest *adj* : dishonest

univarsal *adj* : universal

unknowen *adj* : unknown

unquile *v* : to uncoil

unreconstructed *adj* : said of Southerners who wouldn't reconcile the defeat of the Confederacy in the Civil War

unsighted *adj* : unexpected, unforeseen

untelling *adj* : unknown, unpredictable, erratic

unthoughted *adj* : thought-less, not thought of

untwell *prep* : until

up and died *v* : died <Poor old fella, he ~.>

up-and-gone *adj* : restless, prone to wander, change jobs <He's an ~ feller.>

upbrush *n* : backwoods, hill country

upheaded *adj :* carrying the head erect <She's a fine-looking ~ girl.>

uphelt *v* : uphold, stand up for

up-in-g *adj* : uppity, high class

uppity *adj* : insolent

upscuddle *n* : a quarrel

upsot *adj* : upset

up the creek without a pad-dle *phr* : things look hope-less

up to snuff *adj* : good enough for the job

uptrip *v* : to trip up

uriah *n* : an ignorant, uncouth backwoodsman

urr *n* : sudden impulse, an urge

urs *pron* : us

use *v* : to frequent, loiter

use to could *v* : once able to do something

usings *n* : an amount, as of produce kept for one's own use instead of selling

usted *v* : used <He's ~ to go fishing on Sundays.>

uther *v* : either

- V -

vollydo *n* : a swing or merry-go-round
volunteer *n* : a bastard

vap, vappin' *v* : to run fast
<That ol' hound is sho ~.>
vapors *n* : obscure disease which involves nervous spells, fainting and anemia
vagus *adj* : very important, powerful
varmint *n* : environment
varnish *v* : vanish
varus *adj* : various
vasty *adj* : vast
vault *v* : to conceal in a safe place
vearse *n* : verse
veecious *adj* : vicious
vendue *n* : a public auction
venson *n* : venison
venture *v* : to forbid, not right
veranda *n* : a porch
vice *n* : voice
vicy versy *phr* : vice versa
vigrous, vigrus *adj* : fierce, savage, vicious <That sure is a ~ dog.>
vilyan, villyun *n* : villain
violean *n* : violin
vixen *n* : a mischievous girl
voice *adj* : vile
volentine *n* : valentine

- W -

wad *v* : to embarrass

wade-and-butcher *n* : crude, heavy hunting knife

wag *v* : to carry with difficulty

the Wah *n* : the Civil War — *Var* War Between the States, the War for Southern Independence, the War of Northern Aggression, the War of Secession, and the Cause

wain *n* : wagon

waist *n* : west

waist-baby *n* : baby tall enough when standing to reach one's waist

waiter *n* : best man or bridesmaid

walking in high cotton *v* : become wealthy <He once didn't have a pot to pee in and now he's ~.>

walk in the wind *v* : to walk on air

wall *v* : to roll the eyes to show surprise

Wampus Kitty *n* : a mythical bloodthirsty animal thought to lurk in the wilds

wangs *n* : wings

wan't *v* : wasn't or weren't

wapper-jaw *n* : a projecting under-jaw

wapsy *n* **1:** a debilitation, weakness **2:** a venereal disease

war *n* : wire

ward *n* : word

ware *v* : to warn or make one aware

warloon *n* : a loon

warm *n* : worm

warnet, warnut *n* : walnut

warnt *n* : warrant

warp *v* : to bend, hit, throw

warrant *v* : weren't

warranted *v :* to be arrested on a warrant

wart taker *n* : one who removes warts by charms or incantations

wash-off *n* : a bath

Washtun *n* : Washington

wasper *n* : wasp

wasp's nest *n* : bread made from wheat

wassy *n* : a wasp

waste *v* : to use, spend

water boy *n* : winch with a long cable and bucket to draw water from a deep hollow

water bread *n* : corn bread

water-dog *n* : an old sailor

waterloo bonney *n :* a mythical fowl described as a cross between a chicken and a wild pigeon

water-sobbed *adj* : water soaked

wawk *v* : to walk

waynable *adv* : at the right age to be weaned

weak *n* : wick

weakified *adj* : weak, tired

weakly *adj* : wiggly

weak trembles *n* : weak and shaky from an empty stomach

wear out *v* : to whip thoroughly

weasand *n* : the windpipe

weather-breeder *n* : an unusually fine day

wede *adj* : withered, shriveled up

wedge-floating *adj* : concentrated, strong, usually said of coffee

wedth *n* : width

weed bender *n* : country resident

week *n* : wick of a candle

weep *v* : to droop, bend over, usually said of trees <Snow and ice make cedars ~.>

weepin' *n* : weapon

welkin *n* : the sky

well-day *n* : day when you are well after being sick

werd *v* : worried

wesket *n* : vest

West By God Virginia *n* : West Virginia

wester, westered *v* : to travel or move toward the west

wet down *v* : to rain

wether *n* : a castrated ram

wet-weather horn *n* : a horn on a cow that turns upward

whack   1: *n* a bargain, an agreement, a lie **2:** *v* : to exaggerate, tell a tall tale

whang up *v* : to patch or repair a garment hurriedly

what all *n* : everything, all, an emphatic term

what it is *phr* : what is it?

what's to pay *phr* : what's the matter?

wheat bread, white bread *n* : bread made from wheat flour

whelp *n* : welt, wale

whet a banner *v* : make a loud noise with a whetstone while sharpening a scythe

whet rock *n* : whetstone, grindstone

whey *v* : to thrash, to beat severely

which-a-way *adv* : which
way <~ did he go?>

**which from tother, tother
from which** *phr* : one from
another

whicker 1: *n* whinny **2:** *v* to
whinny

whickerbill *n* : the prepuce or
foreskin

Whiffle-Bird *n* : a legendary
fowl that always flies back-
ward —*Var* Ponjireen,
Bogie-Bird, Fillyloo Crane

whiggered *n* **1:** a beverage
made by adding herbs to fermented whey **2:** a condition
of milk

whindle, whinle *v* : to whine,
to fret

whippoorwill storm *n* : a
storm in the late spring

whip-stitch *n* : a brief interval

every whip-stitch *n* : all the
time

whirp *v* : to whip

whistle-pig *n* : a groundhog

whistle-pig

Whistler *n :* a mythical black
panther that lures timber
workers to their doom by
whistling at them from cedar
thickets

whitecap *n* : a thief

white-eye *adj* : exhausted,
frightened

whitefish *n* : a mushroom

white lightning *n* : moonshine, illegal homemade
whiskey

white-livered *adv* : term of
reproach

whitening *n* : face powder

white trash *n* : lowest class
of whites

white trunk *n* : a white flour
sack carried by a beggar or
tramp

whittaker *n* : a soft felt hat

who laid the chunk *phr* : expression of great approval <He raises hogs ~.>

whole shebang *n* : everything

whole swadget *n* : large amount

whomper-jawed *adj* : distorted, misshapen, applied to inanimate objects as well as people

whoop and a holler *n* : a short, indefinite distance <It's just ~ down this road.>

whoop and hide *n* : a child's game of hide and seek

whoop owl *n* : hoot owl

whopper-jawed *n* : having large or distorted jaws

whup *v* : whip

whuskey *n* : whiskey

widow-bewitched *n* : woman separated from her husband

widow-maker *n* : a big dead limb that falls unexpectedly

wight *n* : a bit

Willipus-Wallipus *n* : a legendary monster

wimbles *n* : a gimlet

Winchester *n* : any repeating rifle with a lever action

wind *v* : to pause for a breath

winder, windah *n* : window

wind-jammer *n* : a teller of tall tales, also blanket-stretcher, windy-spinner,

windy *n* : a tall tale

windy-spinner *n* : a teller of tall tales, also blanket-stretcher, wind-jammer

wing-footed *n* : slue-footed

winter fever *n* : pneumonia

wiping towel *n* : dish towel

wire *n* : daring, shrewdness, wit

wish *v* : to bewitch

wish book *n* : a mail order catalog

wit *adv* : wet

withouten *prep* : without

wizzen *n* : the windpipe

woobles *n* : feeble-mindedness, idiocy, foolishness

woodgy *adv* : hair tumbled and tousled about

wood's colt *n* : bastard, born out of wedlock

wool *v* **1:** to tussle with **2:** to worry

wool-hat boys *n* **1:** small farmers, tenant farmers, share croppers **2:** mountain men of lower Appalachians

wooly-headed *n* : an impassable thicket of laurel or rhododendron

woosh *n* : wish

wo' out *v* : exhausted

wope *interj* : a mild exclamation indicating surprise

work-brickle *adj* : industrious, anxious to work

workies *n* : working people

work on *v* : to castrate

worm-fence *n* : rail fence erected in a zig-zag fashion

worm-rail *n* : bottom rail of a worm-fence

worration, worryation *n* : worry, annoyance, a blend of worry and botheration

worried *v* : tired

worrisome *n* : wearisome; causing worry

wo'th *n* : worth

Wowzer *n* : a legendary super panther that kills cows and horses by biting their heads off

wozzen *n* : woozen, the gullet

wrang *v* : wrung

wranglesome *adj* : quarrelsome

wrap-rascal *n* : a kind of overcoat

writ *v* : wrote, written

writhen *v* : twisted

wrop *v* : wrap

wudget *n* : a wad, pad, or bundle

wudn't *v* : wasn't

wunk *v* : winked

wunnet *n* : walnut

wush *n* : wish

wusser *adj* : worser, worse

wust *adv* : worst

wut *n* : mistake, blunder

wuth *n* : worth

wum *n* : worm

- Y -

yaffle *n* : armful

yahoo *n* **1:** a rough, brutal, uncouth character **2:** a greenhorn, a back-country lout, an uncouth backwoodsman

yale *n* : yell

y'all *pron* : you all

yaller *n* : yellow

yaller-belly *n* : small fish

yaller patch *n* : thicket of laurel

yaller yam *n* : sweet potato

yam *n* : sweet potato

yander *adj* : yonder

yankeefied *adj* : characteristic of a Yankee

Yankee-trick *n* : a mean, unprincipled action

yanner *adj* : yonder

yanside *prep* : beyond, farther on

yar *adv* : this here, the other <I seen it ~ mornin'.>

yarb, yerb *n* : herb

yard *n* : penis

yard-child *n* : a bastard, an illegitimate child

yard grass *n* : bluegrass used on lawns where this variety is common

yardman *n* : person hired for outside work around the house

yare, yar *n* : year

yark *n* : herb

yarm, yarming *v* **1:** to thrust into, to insert **2:** also to complain <She's all the time ~ about money.>

yarn *v* : to earn

yasm, yassum *phr* : yes ma'am

ye *pron* : you, as in <Thank ~.>

yea-nay *adv* : a person who doesn't know his own mind

yeaning *v* : to bring forth young, as sheep or goat

yearn *v* : earn

ye Gods and little fishes *interj* : exclamation of surprise or wonderment

yelk *n* : yolk

yerb *n* : herb

yerk *v* : to jerk

yester *n* : yesterday <I went to town ~.>

ye-uns *pron* : you

yew shoes *n* : new shoes

yieldy *n* : abundant in quantity

yo, yoe *n* : ewe

yoe-necked *adj* : with a long and hollow neck like a ewe

yokum *n* : a fool

yonkapin *n* : a yellow water lily

yonker-pad *n* : a leaf of a yellow water lily

yooper *interj* : an emphatic affirmative

yopped up *v* : marked, messed <The place is all ~ with cans and bottles.>

you-all *pron* : plural of you

yound *adj* : young

youngling *n* : a child

yourn *pron* : yours, your own

youruns *pron* : your

you'uns *pron* : you-all, you ones

yuther *pron* : other

- Z -

zactly *adv* : exactly

zat *v* : is that <~ so?>

zephyr *n* : a crocheted or knitted diamond-shaped wrap worn over a woman's head and shoulders

zip *n* : molasses

zip-coon *n* : raccoon

zip-coon

zondike *n* : the zodiac

zoon, zune *v* : to go or run fast

Bibliography

Adamas, Ramon F. *Western Words*. Norman, OK: University of Oklahoma Press, 1968.

American Dialect Society. *A Word List from "Bill Arp" and "Rufus Sanders."* American Dialect Society, April 1950.

American Dialect Society. *Word Lists from the South*. American Dialect Society, 1944.

Association of Southern Teachers. *The Second Confederate Speller*. Nashville, TN: Association of Southern Teachers, 1861.

Babington, Mima, and E. Bagby Atwood. *Lexical Usage in Southern Louisiana*. American Dialect Society, 1961.

Barlett, John Russell. *Dictionary of American Words and Phrases*. Boston, MA: Little Brown & Co., 1859.

Berrey, Lester V., and Melvin Van den Bark. *The American Thesaurus of Slang*. Thomas Y. Crowell Company, New York, NY.

Bradley, F. W. *A Word List from South Carolina*. American Dialect Society, May 1946.

Bradley, F. W. *Supplementary List of South Carolina Words and Phrases*. American Dialect Society, April 1954.

Brooks, Cleanth. "The English Language in the South." *A Southern Treasury of Life and Literature*, New York, NY: Scribner, 1937.

Brooks, Cleanth. *The Language of the American South*. Athens, GA: University of Georgia Press, 1985.

Brooks, Cleanth. *The Relation of the Alabama-Georgia Dialect to the Provincial Dialects of Great Britain*. Port Washington, NY: Kennikat Press, 1935.

Brown, Calvin S. *A Glossary of Faulkner's South*. New Haven, CT: Yale University Press, 1976.

Cassidy, Frederic G. *Dictionary of American Regional English*. 5 vols. Cambridge, MA: The Belknap Press of Harvard University Press, 1985.

Craigie, William C., and James R. Hulbert, eds. *A Dictionary of American English on Historical Principles*. Chicago, IL: University of Chicago Press, 1938.

Cunningham, Ray. *Southern Talk, a Disappearing Language*. Asheville, NC: Bright Mountain Books, Inc., 1993.

Davidson, Zeta. *A Word List from the Appalachians and the Piedmont Area of North Carolina*. American Dialect Society, April 1953.

Dial, Wylene P. "The Dialect of the Southern Appalachian People." *West Virginia History Quarterly* (Jan. 1969).

Dillard, J. L. *American Talk*. New York, NY: Random House, 1976.

Eliason, Norman E. Farwell, Harold F., Jr., and J. Karl Nicholas, eds. *Smoky Mountain Voices, A Lexicon of Southern Appalachian Speech*. Lexington, KY: University Press of Kentucky, 1993.

Finkenstaedt, Thomas. *A Chronological English Dictionary*. Heidelberg, Germany: Carl Winter University, 1970.

Flexner, Stuart Berg. *I Hear American Talking*. New York, NY: Simon & Schuster, 1976.

Graves, John Temple. "Southern Speech." *Southern Speech Journal* (Nov. 1938).

Green, B. W. *Word Book of Virginia Folk Speech*. Richmond, VA: W.E. Jones' Sons, 1912.

Hendrickson, Robert. *Whistlin' Dixie, A Dictionary of Southern Expressions*. New York, NY: Facts on File, 1933.

Herman, Lewis, and Marguerite S. Herman. *American Dialects*. New York, NY: Theatre Art Books, 1947.

Kurath, Hans. *A Word Geography of the Eastern United States*. Ann Arbor, MI: University of Michigan Press, 1949.

Kurath, Hans, and Raven I. McDavid, Jr. *The Pronunciation of English in the Atlantic States*. Ann Arbor, MI: The University of Michigan Press, 1961.

Lucke, Jesse Ryon. "A Study of the Virginia Dialect and Its Origin in England." Ph.D. diss., University of Virginia, Charlottesville, 1949.

Major, Clarence, ed. *Dictionary of African-American Slang*. New York, NY: International, 1970.

Mathews, Mitford M., ed. *A Dictionary of Americanisms on Historical Principles*. 2 vols. Chicago, IL: The University of Chicago Press, 1951.

McDavid, Raven I. Jr. "Linguistic Atlas of the Middle and South Atlantic States." *Southern Folklore Quarterly* (Dec. 1948).

McMillan, James B., and Michael B. Montgomery. *Annotated Bibliography of Southern American English*. Coral Gables, FL: University of Miami Press, 1971, 1989.

Mencken, H. L. *The American Language*, 4th ed. New York, NY: Alfred Knopf, Inc., 1936.

Montgomery, Michael, and Guy Bailey. *The Handbook of the Linguistic Atlas of the Gulf States*. Chapel Hill, NC: University of North Carolina Press,1986.

Montgomery, Michael, and Guy Bailey. *The Language Variety in the South*. University, AL: University of Alabama Press, 1986.

Newton, David W. *Voices Along the Border: Cultural Identity, Social Authority and Idea of Language in the Antebellum South, 1830-1860*. Atlanta, GA: Emory University, 1993.

Nixon, Phyllis. *A Glossary of Virginia Words*. American Dialect Society, 1946.

Randolph, Vance, and George P. Wilson. *Down in the Holler, A Gallery of Ozark Folk Speech*. Norman, OK: University of Oklahoma Press, 1953.

Read, William Alexander. *The Southern R*. Baton Rouge, LA: Independent Press, 1910.

Shewmake, Edwin F. "English Pronunciation in Virginia." The University of Virginia, 1928.

Shores, David L. *Tangier Island: Place, People and Talk*. Newark, DE: University of Delaware Press, 2002

Thornton, Richard H. *American Glossary*. 3 vols. New York, NY: Frederick Ungar Publishing Co., 1962.

Tidwell, James Nathan. *A Word List from West Texas*. American Dialect Society, April 1949.

Wentworth, Harold. *American Dialect Dictionary*. New York, NY: Thomas Y. Crowell Co., 1944.

Wentworth, Harold, and Stuart Flexner. *Dictionary of American Slang*. New York, NY: Thomas Y. Crowell Co., 1958.

Wilder, Roy, Jr., *You All Spoken Here*. New York, NY: Viking Penguin, Inc., 1984.

Wilson, Charles R., and William Ferris, eds. *Encyclopedia of Southern Culture*. Chapel Hill, NC: University of North Carolina Press, 1989.

Wolfram, Walt, and Donna Christian. *Appalachian Speech*. Arlington, VA.: Center for Applied Linguistics, 1976.

Woodard, C. M. *A Word List from Virginia and North Carolina*. American Dialect Society, November 1946.

Wood, Gordon R. *Vocabulary Change*. Carbondale, IL: Southern Illinois University Press, 1971.

Wood, Gordon R. *Word Distribution in the Interior South*. American Dialect Society, April 1961.

Wright, Joseph. *English Dialect Dictionary*. 6 vols. London, England: Oxford University Press, 1898.

Wright, Thomas. *Dictionary of Obsolete and Provincial English*. 2 vols. London, England: Henry G. Bohn, 1857.

About the Author

Thomas W. Howard is the descendant of 17th-century Virginia colonists. Now retired, he graduated from the University of Richmond and worked as an editor and reporter for the *Richmond Times-Dispatch* for almost 40 years. He has contributed as a humor columnist, book reviewer, and feature writer to more than 30 newspapers and magazines, including *Fortune, Time, Newsweek, Chemical Week*, and *McGraw Hill World News*. His book, *Black Voyage*, about the Atlantic slave trade (Little Brown), was ranked by *The School Library Journal* as one of the ten best juvenile books of 1971. *The Dixie Dictionary* is the result of more than 30 years spent collecting and studying Southern words and phrases.